Spanish Peaks

Talked to the God of Hosts about the Native American
situation and he said everything's a matter of time,
that though it's small comfort the ghosts have already
nearly destroyed us with the ugliness we've become,
that in a few hidden glades in North America
half-human bears still dance in imperfect circles.

—Jim Harrison, *After Ikkyu and Other Poems*

Spanish Peaks

LAND AND LEGENDS

BY CONGER BEASLEY JR.

PHOTOGRAPHS BY BARBARA SPARKS

WITH A FOREWORD BY ANN H. ZWINGER

University Press of Colorado

Published by the University Press of Colorado
5589 Arapahoe Avenue, Suite 206C
Boulder, Colorado 80303

 The University Press of Colorado is a proud member of
the Association of American University Presses.

The University Press of Colorado is a cooperative publishing enterprise supported, in part, by
Adams State College, Colorado State University, Fort Lewis College, Mesa State College, Metro-
politan State College of Denver, University of Colorado, University of Northern Colorado,
University of Southern Colorado, and Western State College of Colorado.

∞ The paper used in this publication meets the minimum requirements of the American
National Standard for Information Sciences—Permanence of Paper for Printed Library Materials.
ANSI Z39.48-1992

Library of Congress Cataloging-in-Publication Data

Beasley, Conger.
  Spanish Peaks : land and legends / by Conger Beasley, Jr. ; photography by Barbara Sparks ;
foreword by Ann H. Zwinger.
      p. cm.
Includes bibliographical references.
  ISBN-10: 0-87081-604-7 (alk. paper)
  ISBN-13: 978-0-87081-853-0 (pbk : alk. paper)
  ISBN-10: 0-87081-853-8 (pbk : alk. paper)
  1. Spanish Peaks Wilderness (Colo.)—History. 2. Legends—Colorado—Spanish Peaks
Wilderness. I. Title.
  F782.S76 B43 2001
  978.8'5—dc21
                                                                                    2001000750

Cover design by Laura Furney
Text design by Daniel Pratt

15   14   13   12   11   10   09   08   07   06   10 9 8 7 6 5 4 3 2 1

For Tom Doerk

For Kathryn Beamer

And for Paige, Brooke,
Henry, Jane, Chloe, and Ike

Contents

Foreword

When we moved to Colorado Springs forty years ago, the Spanish Peaks lay on the horizon as I looked south out my kitchen window. A midwesterner like Beasley, I was fascinated by being able to see mountains nearly a hundred miles away and by the paired peaks. I observed those mountains in many weathers, and so strong was the image that even when we had upslope or winter storms I somehow retained them in my mind's eye. Questions about the Spanish Peaks drifted through my mind, some of them answered, but I never gained a sense of their whole majesty. This book by Conger Beasley and Barbara Sparks does just that—answers all those questions and gives a comprehensive account of their presence.

A theory exists that the Greeks only built their temples where twin rises were on the horizon; perhaps that pairing of crests evokes a deep-seated response in humans, one of which we are only dimly aware other than feeling a pull, a wish to know more, to understand a landform that speaks subtly but strongly, perhaps even erotically, given the Spanish Peaks' other names and their unavoidable resemblance to the well-endowed female form.

More and more we are becoming conscious of the landscape of home and how it affects our lives. And more and more it becomes important to examine the landscape that surrounds us in some detail for the larger understanding this affords us. In times that move quickly and when important events are disposed of in sound bites, understanding the place where we live or to which we feel an attachment is stabilizing and reassuring. Such an examination never ends but always continues to reveal the richness of a landscape psyche. I hope this combination of writer and photographer exploring a specific landscape in depth will entice others to do the same.

The area around the Spanish Peaks that Beasley and Sparks have studied is by no means small; the terrain combines 13,000-foot peaks with foothills sloping into plains, each an ecosystem of great variety and richness. The joining of plains and mountains forms an ecotone, a place of overlapping plant and animal species that generally has a greater richness than either of the zones it combines. This quality alone makes the Spanish Peaks a fascinating area to photograph and write about.

Author's and photographer's careful perusal of landform and landscape, of people and land use, of a range of human experience and particular knowledge, and how the people who actually live there today feel about the Spanish Peaks forms a near-definitive study of a clear and present landform. This is an outstanding book of research and exploration, of powerful landscape and people's relationship to it. They have explored the ground and gotten the message through their own feet, have flown over it and seen how the landforms fit into each other, the jigsaw puzzle of valleys and slopes made whole. Sparks's photographs illuminate the text and add their own perceptions of time and place in sharp and careful shadows, in faces that map a lifetime. The combination is serendipitous. The result is a book that honors a remarkable landmark in Colorado, that pays homage to the unmistakable and magnificent Spanish Peaks.

—Ann H. Zwinger, Colorado Springs

Acknowledgments

We wish to extend our heartfelt thanks to the following: Tom Doerk, La Veta Bookstore; Nancy Christofferson; Cindy Pierotti, librarian, La Veta Library; Gail Ritter, Claudia Capps, and the Territorial Daughters of Southern Colorado; Sara Murphy, librarian, Trinidad Library; Floyd Chavez, rancher, Weston; Will Prator, La Veta; Rae and John Albright and their sons George and Loren, ranchers in La Veta; Lucy and Joe Garbo, Trinidad; Anne Lucero and her son Gordon, Trujillo Creek; Jim Young, pilot, Colorado Springs; Colleen Oquist, United States Forest Service, La Junta; Trinidad and William Roybal, Pueblo; Bob Kennemer, Apishapa Canyon guide, La Veta; Larry Harris, geologist, La Veta; Bob Tapia, Cokedale.

We would also like to thank the Jesuit priests of Holy Trinity Church, Trinidad: Fathers Bob Hagan, Mark MacKenzie, and Gene Renard. We also thank Reverend Maurice Gallagher of Avondale.

We wish to recognize the help and assistance of Carolyn Brown, Pam Munroe, Sandy Hackbarth, Leo Sagar, Dolores Vialpando, Albert Mattie, Julia Silver, Tom and Vicki Zamborelli, Clayton Sparks, Stuart Dodge, Dan Norton, Ken Sparks, Betsy Beasley, and Bill Beasley; Mark Miller, archaeologist, Comanche National Grasslands; Cathy Wright, Taylor Museum Curator, Colorado Springs; Chris Huffman, First National Bank, Trinidad; Ginny Kiefer, curator, Special Collections, Tutt Library, Colorado College; Liz Lewis, Special Collections, Tutt Library, Colorado College; Jenny Guy, manager, Colorado College Bookstore.

We are indebted to Andrea Sparks for her rendering of the Spanish Peaks' region map.

Finally, we thank Luther Wilson, Darrin Pratt, and Laura Furney of the University Press of Colorado.

Barbara Sparks was aided in her research and photography by a grant from the Colorado Endowment for the Humanities in Denver.

The chapter "Among the Penitentes" was first published in the Colorado Springs *Independent,* April 20–26, 2000.

Listing of Variant Spellings

What follows is a listing of variant spellings, descriptions, and definitions of the two mountains popularly known as the Spanish Peaks.

Wahatoya (Breasts of the World)
Huatolla
Huajatolla
Guajatolla
Los Juajatoyas
Wah-to-yah
Las Cumbres Españolas (the Spanish Peaks)
Dos Hermanos (Two Brothers)
Twin Peaks
Siamese Peaks
Double Mountain
Dream Mountain
Los Tetones
Mamas del Mundo (Breasts of the World)

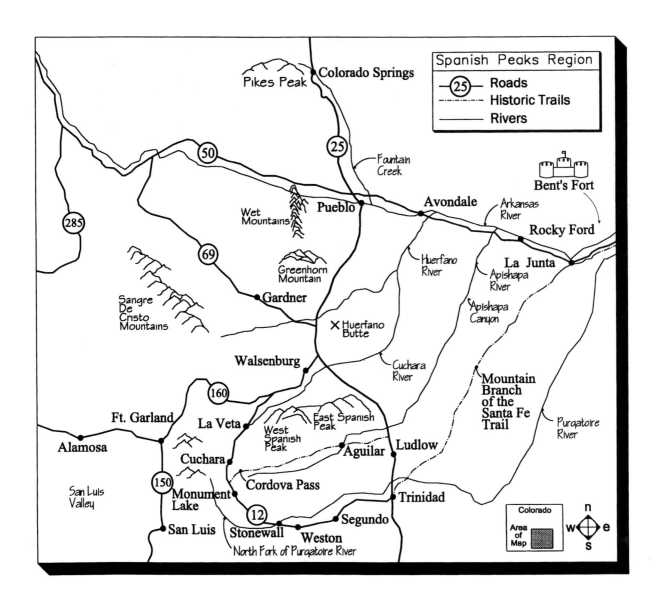

Spanish Peaks

Lonesome Water

Many years ago, when the earth was very young, a stream of water flowing down from the Sangre de Cristo range west of the Spanish Peaks fell in love with a little green valley basking in the cool blue shadow of the great Stonewall. The water refused to run off somewhere else; instead, it sank into the ground and settled around the roots of the wild roses that grew on the valley floor. To this day, the water bubbles in little springs between the rocky ledges enclosing the valley. It has a distinct peppermint flavor and looks like green ice, and once a person has tasted it, he never wants to leave the valley.

1
First View

It must have been sometime in the 1970s. I was driving from Kansas City, Missouri, to Palm Desert, California, across the long sweeping glide of eastern Colorado, looking for a different path through the Rockies. I wanted to avoid the big cities, so I angled southwest out of La Junta, away from Denver and Colorado Springs, thinking that at Walsenburg I would maintain a westerly course on Highway 160 over La Veta Pass into the San Luis Valley. A few miles out of La Junta I saw these two peaks off to the left, seemingly connected, a double-humped formation rising in isolated splendor several miles east of the formidable phalanx of the Sangre de Cristo Mountains. I fumbled for the map, spread it across the steering wheel, but they weren't marked or identified. As time passed I watched them grow bigger; an hour later, gassing up in Walsenburg—nearly within their shadow—I asked the attendant, "What do you call those two mountains over there?"

The attendant took a bite of a Snickers bar and handed me my change. Despite the warm temperature he wore a fur cap and paint-spattered wool shirt, lace-up shoes, and no socks; his cheeks were fuzzed with whitish stubble. "They're the Spanish Peaks. Least that's what we call them here. Dos Hermanos. Wa-too-yuh. They got all sorts of names."

Certain landscapes cast certain spells. The reasons for this are complex, an intermingling of aesthetic appeal and emotional response. Forms and figures swathed in color touch responsive chords that trigger a charge of strong feelings—feelings that suggest a deeper identification with a specific terrain than can be initially explained. As a native midwesterner I'm drawn to smooth, unruffled surfaces, but these peaks, rising in solitary

Spanish Peaks, late afternoon.

grandeur with the leading edge of the High Plains lapping their lower slopes, caught my fancy. Here at the portal to the southern Rockies they stood forth like sentinels. How could you pass this way and not pay them notice?

Several miles west of Walsenburg, on Highway 160 leading up toward La Veta Pass, I pulled the car over and stepped out. To the south the peaks rose in full profile, filling the frame of the horizon. It was early June, and the meadows and pastures nudging the slopes were just beginning to green out. Dark groves of conifers glowed higher up. The faint track of a road looped away from the highway and dipped down through a lush valley cut by a slim river, finally connecting with the north edge of a little town marked La Veta on the map. The road then wound around a slope leading up to a gap between the peaks and a range of snow-dappled mountains to the west. Now where does that go? I wondered. I remember feeling an actual physical tug as I watched the road, Colorado Highway 12, disappear into the notch. Was that town over there like the one I'd been looking for all my adult life? An imaginary town filled with people the age of my parents when they were young, speaking in melodious voices? More of a settlement than a town, rough-hewn and wild, with smoke curling up from countless fires, children speeding about on bicycles, women in long dresses and soft felt caps festooned with colorful feathers, men in worsted suits, gold watch fobs spangling their stout waists, sporting broad-brimmed hats they tip to every-one in an affable manner. A town with no franchise joints, little neon or plastic, brick-fronted stores, wide, dusty, unpaved streets shaded by leafy elms and sycamores, birds clustered in the branches, horses stabled in the backyards, goats and cows grazing in a grassy commons on the outskirts.

I must have stood there next to my car looking out at the apparition of the peaks and valley for quite some time. No, no, impossible, I thought, I'm day-tripping again. Some roads beckon with a magic of their own, and at the center of that magic is an image of how we think life should be, and the source of that image is usually a notion—intuitive or acquired, ideal-ized to be sure—of how things would look and feel if only we were in charge. And here it was, I thought, a scene that only the gods could con-coct, which already had captured my complete attention, backed by a pair of snow-capped mountains seemingly fused at the hip, floating under their own power through an ethereal blue sky. This is it, I thought, the incarna-tion of the notion that has dogged me all my life, the actual fact.

But instead of checking right then and there, I got back in the car and drove to California and didn't come back to the Spanish Peaks for many years. It didn't matter. I wasn't in a hurry. I knew the reality would never correspond to the image in my head. It never does. And yet, misleading though they may be, such images are never really proven wrong. They're merely dismissed or excused or tucked away in a special place where they linger with haunting persistence, like the warble of a mourning dove on a warm summer evening.

Paradise

At the beginning of time, a kind of paradise on earth flourished at the foot of the Spanish Peaks, where no person suffered pain or cold or was even unhappy. This blissful state continued until the gods grew bored and decided that this beautiful place should be like any other. Later, the rain gods took control of the peaks and began generating dark clouds and dispatching them all over the world. A new era began, which the rain gods proudly extolled. "Huajatolla are two breasts as round as a woman's," they declared, "and all living things on earth, mankind, beasts, and plants, derive their sustenance from that source. The clouds are born there, and without clouds there is no rain, and when no rain falls we have no food, and without food we must perish."

2
West Spanish Peak

The trail up to the tree line of West Spanish Peak was gradual and not too strenuous, and after breakfast we started out from the campground at Cordova Pass (10,233 ft.) and sauntered along at a smooth, easy pace. At one point, crossing a grassy meadow splashed with colorful wildflowers, we caught a spectacular view—northwest toward the neighboring peaks of the Sangre de Cristos, Mount Blanca in particular, looming over the sandy flats of the San Luis Valley; southeast across the Apishapa River Valley, the foothills ladling down toward the town of Aguilar and the distant flatlands, glimmering in the soft morning light. Then the clouds slipped our way, cutting off the view, an unfavorable omen; if there were clouds when we reached the tree line, we'd have to scrub our attempt to ascend the west peak (13,626 ft.). The trail to the top is difficult to follow; it's hand over hand up a precipitous slope (70 degrees at times) of cracked and broken rock to a final ridgeline slanting to the summit. Clouds dampened the rocks and made them a lot slicker than they would be on a cloudless day. We were a quartet of enthusiastic middle-agers out for a look at one-half of a twin mountain complex that beckoned to each of us in deeply personal ways.

Aspen, spruce, and ponderosa gave way gradually to smaller groves of fir, bristlecone, and limber pine. We saw mountain bluebirds, nutcrackers, chickadees, and gray jays. Turkey vultures wheeled in steady arcs on warm updrafts from the lower valleys. Abert's squirrels, with their pointy ears, chattered vexatiously. There were no bears. Undoubtedly, they were here; a party of four laboring uphill, pointing out stuff to one another, makes a lot of racket, and if there were bears, they had plenty of time to hunker down.

Bristlecone pine.

I dawdled behind my three companions, taking my time, playing little mental tricks to maintain my uphill momentum, uttering a chant in sync with my breathing, a kind of aspirated rasp that helped pull me along. It was nice to sidle along the flank of the big peak, rubbing both shoulders against the high banks of some of the switchbacks, making contact, getting tactile. The Spanish Peaks stand side by side (though some say one follows the other in a westerly direction) south of the little town of La Veta, Colorado. The peaks are igneous intrusions that pushed their way up through Cretaceous and Tertiary sedimentary layers around 26 to 22 million years ago, after most of the rest of the Colorado Rockies had been formed. Erosion removed the overlying sedimentary layers, exposing the granite summits. Technically, because they were formed by upwelling molten rock that never erupted, they're known as stocks; and although I have no way of proving this, I think the fact that they didn't blow is in part responsible for the peculiar aura they radiate, the power they give off. All that force impacted within a pair of sturdy pinnacles, visible for 80 miles out on the plains, beacon and guidepost for countless generations of Indians, Hispanics, and Anglos. No wonder there're so many stories about them.

Another salient feature are the dikes that radiate down from the upper slopes. As the magma punched its way up from chambers deep inside the earth, it fractured the surface. Molten material rushed into the cracks, spreading down and out, finally cooling and eroding into the thin, membranous blades, or "dikes," we see prominently displayed on all sides of the peaks. In fact, the Spanish Peaks boast the most spectacular display of radial dikes in the United States. Dozens of dikes of varying sizes ripple like vertical ribbons down the topmost slopes, some a mere few inches wide, others 30 feet thick or more.

Of all the phenomena in nature, the most difficult to conceptualize is the creation of the landforms we see around us. A time-lapse camera might serve to illustrate the rise of mountains such as the Spanish Peaks, but how to visualize the gradual wearing away of these forms over an infinitesimal span of time? No satisfactory graphic can convey that transformation. Watching paint dry on a blank wall seems positively frantic by comparison. The human imagination simply cannot grasp such an event. Maybe once upon a time when people lived their entire lives in this milieu, they might have achieved an intuitive inkling of what a mountain felt like. But we weekend enthusiasts don't have much of a clue. We drive up to a point as high as our vehicles can take us, lock the doors, strap on our water bottles, slap on the sunblock, and start up. The transition from insulated comfort to maximum exposure is pathetically brief. We pray our hearts don't sputter and fail, and with that thought consuming our consciousness we toil to the top in a fidgety, paranoic mind-set, the same mind-set that animates our lives back down in the hectic congestion of the cities we inhabit.

That morning, after about an hour and a half of steady climbing, the trees commenced to shrink and thin, patches of whitish sky appeared, and our little party emerged onto a cracked and broken shelf at the base of the summit of the west peak. The clouds closed down; outside the tree cover the wind picked up, sending veils of creamy mist swirling over the shattered face of the summit. "Doesn't look good," photographer Barbara Sparks muttered. No, it certainly doesn't, a voice echoed in my head. The way up was steep, a prodigious crawl of an additional thousand feet. The jumble of rocks rising toward the top felt slick. Once we got there, if we got there, the view would be totally obscured.

It gets easier to rationalize critical decisions involving strenuous exercise as one gets older. My gout is acting up, my joints ache, my sinuses feel musty and plugged; but then, conversely, age makes us feel more vulnerable. I can die at any moment, not just from an accident but from a major breakdown of my functioning parts.

I sat down on a rock and gazed up the steep incline that disappeared behind a ghostly curtain of condensed moisture. I'll never know what the world looks like from the top of this mountain, a voice grumbled inside my head.

Of course you will, came the reply. Come back in a few days and the clouds will be gone, and you can inch your way to the top like a caterpillar up a length of frayed rope, and from that coveted perch you can shout your exultation for all the world to hear. Larry Harris, a geologist friend who

Tree limit, West Spanish Peak.

lives down in La Veta, once climbed both the west and east peaks in a single day.

It's nice to have made it this far, I concluded, and offered a pinch of tobacco at the base of a rocky outcropping. Then I started down after the others, glancing over my shoulder, hoping for a glimpse of the shattered crown of this imposing peak, which like a persistent dream had insinuated itself under the skin of my consciousness.

Cuchara Pass

In the old days Indians gathered at the top of Cuchara Pass to swap stories of brave deeds. After a huge feast, warriors danced around the fire acting out their deeds. The Indian with the most expressive dance was given an eagle feather and asked to repeat the dance again and again. As he circled the fire, fanning his face with the feather, he rose in a spiral until he was as high as the tops of the trees. At that moment both he and the rising spiral of his dance congealed into a spruce tree. After many years, what had been a vast open space at the top of the pass became filled with trees.

3
From the Air

The sun rose just moments after the single-engine Piper Malibu lifted off the runway at the Colorado Springs airport and banked east into a glorious effusion of pinkish-orange light that lit up the flat horizon and filled the interior of the fuselage with a warm sugary glow. The plane, piloted by Jim Young, a friend of Barbara Sparks's, wheeled south-southwest toward the Spanish Peaks, 80 miles away. Barbara, wearing earphones, sat in the copilot's seat, camera in hand. I sat in the passenger cabin on the starboard side, looking out the window. A few minutes later, as we approached Pueblo, Colorado, the peaks took on a new configuration, that of a headless woman with prominent breasts lying on her back, feet and torso merging indistinguishably with the north-south axis of the Culebra Range of the Sangre de Cristo Mountains.

Fountain Creek, after first splashing down Ute Pass behind Colorado Springs, flows south along the edge of the foothills to a confluence with the Arkansas in downtown Pueblo. We passed over the power plant with its twin striped smokestacks, then over a series of ripply ridges matted along their smooth backs with masses of piñon and juniper. Four rivers drain the Spanish Peaks region—the Huerfano, Cuchara, Apishapa, and Purgatoire. They leak out of the mountains through rock-choked channels, slicing through the foothills onto the plains, curving east-northeast to empty into the Arkansas, the region's major drainage. Greenhorn Mountain, north of the Spanish Peaks, with its flat, hulking profile, was easy to identify; at its foot in 1789, Spanish commander Juan Bautista de Anza encountered Comanche chief Cuerno Verde (after whom the mountain is named) and killed him and many of his followers, bringing a measure of

Mamas del Mundo from
confluence of Cuchara and
Huerfano Rivers.

peace to southern Colorado and northern New Mexico for the first time
in a century.

People call the plains flat, but this close to the mountains they're not;
they exhibit far more topographical variety than is commonly supposed.
The massive upthrust of the Sangre de Cristos caused the adjacent flatlands
to buckle and fold, squeezing up knobs, buttes, and bulges. The slanting
light from the rising sun cast each protuberance into stark relief, splashing
slick, dark shadows across the smooth turtle-backed humps between the
drainages. These shadows became more pronounced as we approached the
peaks from the north-northeast. From an elevation of 15,000 feet, the bald
summits of the double mountain looked deeply fissured and grooved; inky
shadows swept down the forested north-facing slopes to the edge of the
grasslands of the Cuchara Valley.

West Spanish Peak presented a more elongated profile than its coun-
terpart, which rose to its crest in a concerted, conical thrust. (It must be
tougher to climb, I opined from the pressurized comfort of the purring
plane, forgetting my own thwarted attempt to scale the west peak a few
months before.) The middle slopes of both peaks were forested with a furry
covering of trees, highlighted in late September with splashes of yellow
aspen and the bluish tint of Engelmann spruce. The long, dragon-backed

west peak loomed larger; it bore a wider base, more extensive ridgelines, ample areas of cracked and shattered scree, plus myriad chutes, gouged by avalanches, trailing down through the trees. By comparison, the east peak (12,683 ft.) seemed smaller and more self-contained. The peaks of both mountains this radiant morning were dusted with snow on their north summits. An array of vertical dikes fanned out from their sides like lengths of light-colored string, starting above the tree line in some cases and bumping down through the forests all the way to the flatlands.

Far to the south, at the foot of Raton Pass marking the Colorado–New Mexico border, the town of Trinidad sparkled in the morning light like bits of splintered glass. I could see the threads of the Apishapa and Purgatoire Rivers trickling down from the heights, the first from deep within the peaks, the second from the Culebra Range of the Sangre de Cristos to the west. Together these two streams and their tributaries carve gentle valleys through sedimentary layers laid down during the Mesozoic era, 80 to 100 million years ago.

For a full thirty minutes we flew around the peaks, we flew over them, Barbara clicking away from the copilot's seat, me sliding back and forth to peer out both sets of portholes on the right- and left-hand sides. With the invention of the airplane, humankind acquired the capacity for aerial perspective that once belonged exclusively to birds and shamans. Here we were on this beautiful morning, cruising over these stony crowns, looking looking looking, trying within a brief glimpse of time to affix these dazzling images permanently upon our consciousness. And then Jim brought the

Twin peaks, twin shadows.

Dikes radiating down from East
Peak.

aircraft (call name *Romeo Tango*) around in a slow, wheeling turn and guided
it between the peaks, smack over the forested saddle, down across the
piney green cleavage, between the legendary Mamas del Mundo, and I
heard myself yipping like a terrier, "yip! yip! yip!" as we roared out over the
north-facing slopes spilling from the shadows into the sunlit brilliance of
the meadows and pastures of the Cuchara Valley.

At 17,000 feet, like peeping Toms we could see over the long ripply
summits of the Culebras immediately to the west into the wide sandy depths
of the San Luis Valley. Blanca Peak (14,345 ft.) loomed to the northwest in
monolithic splendor. Off to the left I spotted the curve marking the heights
of La Veta Pass. So much terrain encompassed in a single glance, so much
history and lore—Fort Garland, Kit Carson, Great Sand Dunes, the hamlet
of San Luis. And on the east side Mount Mestas (named after a local World

Close-up, East Spanish Peak.

Huerfano Butte.

War II hero), La Veta, the prinkly ribbon of the Cuchara River, the former coal-mining emporium of Walsenburg.

Jim banked the plane to the right, and we picked up the flash of the Huerfano River trickling down the backside of Blanca Peak and across the mouth of the Wet Mountain Valley. We followed it northeast as it slipped through the foothills, widening appreciably with each mile. As it widened, revealing sandy shoals and islands, it generated more cultivation: fields, pastures, houses, roads. Early pioneers such as George Simpson soon discovered that crops and forage could be grown along the riverine systems linking mountains and plains in this part of the world but not on the plains themselves, which were suitable only for grazing.

And then, off the right wing, the tiny cinderous cone of Huerfano ("Orphan") Butte, an isolated knob of intrusive igneous rock that rises a hundred feet high, composed of black rock so hard it rings like metal when struck with a hammer. A solitary, weathered, volcanic plug that pokes up like a discolored blister, landmark in its own diminutive way for generations of Indians, soldiers, and settlers.

And then in for a landing at Pueblo, followed by a hearty breakfast at the airport restaurant. *Romeo Tango* was left on the tarmac to have its tanks topped out with aviation fuel while we downed coffee and huevos rancheros and spoke glowingly of the ride and what we had just seen.

Cuchara

Cuchara is the Spanish word for *spoon*. It is said that both the river and the valley received their names when early explorers found ancient spoons along the banks of the river. Others say the name was bestowed because of the spoonlike shape of the valley, the handle starting high up in the mountains, the spoon part opening on the lowlands where the town of La Veta lies today. Still others claim that long ago one of the giants who roamed the earth put down his spoon after a heavy rain, leaving an indelible impression that has never gone away.

4
La Veta

There's something appealing about the town of La Veta (pop. 800). Only two of the streets are paved; the rest are dirt. The town is crisscrossed with alleys, always a good sign—thoroughfares for transient animals, secret routes for playful kids. Trees shade most of the streets—ash, elm, locust, sycamore, box elder. The sun in this part of the world shines with dazzling intensity through a thin cushion of clear air, and it's best to cover up during the day with a hat and long sleeves. The businesses along Main Street—Charlie's, the Covered Wagon, the realty offices and gift shops—sport simple, unpretentious fronts fashioned of native sandstone. People come and go with an old-fashioned languor that seems blissfully devoid of the kind of electronic jitter that animates the citizens of Denver and Colorado Springs. It's a congenial town, people-oriented, scaled in such a way to accommodate human quirks and feelings. Amid the boom currently disrupting much of the Front Range from Pueblo north to Fort Collins, it retains a distinct small-town mystique.

The cultural center of La Veta lies in Francisco Fort, a low, squat, adobe redoubt, now the town's historical museum, built in the 1860s by three men of diverse backgrounds: John Francisco, Henry Daigre, and Hiram Vasquez.

John Francisco was born in Virginia in 1820. At age nineteen he led a team of twenty-five ox-drawn wagons along the Santa Fe Trail. He went to Taos for a while, where he supplied the U.S. Army with hay, grain, and beef. In 1859 he was appointed sutler (civilian supplier) at Fort Garland, in the San Luis Valley. At some point he crossed the Sangre de Cristo Mountains and viewed the Cuchara Valley, about which he reportedly remarked, "I have found my home. This is paradise enough for me."

1899 Inn, Main Street, La Veta. Used as a hospital during aftermath of Ludlow Massacre, April 1914.

Starting in 1862, in concert with Henry Daigre, he oversaw the construction of the fort that bears his name. The land was purchased from Cornelio Vigil and Ceran St. Vrain, the sole proprietors of a huge land grant in their names. The size of the grant boggles the imagination today. It stretched east to the Kansas border, north to the line of the Arkansas River, west to the Sangre de Cristos, and south to New Mexico—around 4 million acres.

To successfully claim title to any part of a land grant, fields had to be cleared and cultivated, dwellings erected, and the land continuously occupied. John Francisco was haughty and aristocratic; much as he might dislike sharing his grand estate with anyone, it was obvious that one man couldn't possibly provide the necessary labor to establish a viable claim to such a vast tract. And so he hired Henry Daigre to oversee the work.

Daigre was born in Quebec in 1832. At age six months his mother died, and his father abandoned him. A kindly uncle saw to his upbringing, and after spending his first fifteen years in Quebec, he went to New York, where he worked in a store.

He bounced around the country as a young man, working at different jobs—for the railroad in Louisiana, as a brakeman on the Ohio and Mississippi Railroad, as a deckhand on boats between St. Louis and New

Sandstone ice house, built 1895. Today a carpenter shop.

Orleans. In 1860 he drove an ox team to Fort Garland, where he became acquainted with John Francisco. Recognizing his talents and energetic disposition, Francisco recommended that Daigre join him in the Cuchara Valley, where he was planning to build a *placita,* a protective compound enclosed with an adobe wall.

The two men hired a team of over twenty skilled workers to construct the compound. One of the men was barely twenty years old—tall, serious, immensely capable, with shining blue eyes. His name was Hiram Vasquez. Born in St. Louis, the stepson of mountain man Louis Vasquez, young Hiram had been kidnapped by a band of Shoshone Indians at Fort Bridger, Wyoming, in 1847 when he was four years old. Washakie, chief of the Shoshone, took a fancy to the blue-eyed boy and slipped off with him into the wilderness.

For several years young Hiram lived with the Shoshone, where he was well treated. He learned their ways and spoke their language. In 1852, when he was nine, the band made a trip to the mountains near present-day Salt Lake City, which was then little more than a collection of motley houses and stores. Young Hiram begged to go, but the Indians refused, so he sneaked off and made his way to town. While roaming the streets, dressed only in a breechclout, his hair decorated with silver conchas and a plait of horsehair, he was recognized as a white person and immediately detained. Someone remembered the little Anglo boy who'd been abducted years before at Fort Bridger, and he was returned to his family.

Hiram spent the rest of his youth with his original family in western Missouri. With his young life already colored by a fabulous array of experiences, it was only natural that he would return to the West as an outfitter on the Santa Fe Trail. He passed through the Spanish Peaks region several times on the way to Taos and each time felt himself drawn to it more deeply. When the opportunity occurred to work with John Francisco and Henry Daigre on the construction of Francisco Fort, young Hiram, then barely twenty years old, signed on. "Almost from his first glimpse of the luxuriant Cuchara Valley," says his biographer, Zella Rae Albright, "Hiram . . . became firmly convinced that here in this beautiful land he would find not only peace of mind, but also the meaning of, and the reason for, his very existence" (Albright, p. 103).

Francisco Fort, later called Francisco Plaza, was built of adobe in the shape of a square enclosing a well. The walls were 2 feet thick. The square measured about a hundred feet on each side. A heavy double-doored gate marked the entrance on the north side. Wagons and livestock could easily be accommodated within the walls. The single-story buildings were roofed with thick slabs of dirt; a parapet surrounding the buildings enabled riflemen to fire over the tops of the walls. The fort served as a trading post, shelter, and stopping place for scouts, trappers, prospectors, and settlers. It later became the focal point of the new town of La Veta ("the Vein," for the long, whitish-colored dikes that radiate down from the nearby Spanish Peaks).

La Veta ("the Vein"). Dike glowing
in late afternoon sun.

In the spring of 1863 the team of twenty-one men working on the fort was besieged by a war party of Muache Utes led by their principal chief, Kaniache. The Utes approached early one morning but were detected by a sentry in time for the rest of the men to corral the working stock and position themselves behind the protective walls. A few well-placed shots temporarily cooled Kaniache's enthusiasm for an all-out charge, and he sat down with his men to feast on a bevy of slain beeves, confident the compelling need for water would eventually drive the beleaguered whites into the open. Unbeknownst to Kaniache, the fort was provisioned with plenty of water, as well as ample ammunition, beans, corn, flour, and slabs of fresh meat. Nonetheless, the situation was grim, and John Francisco asked for a volunteer to ride for help to Fort Lyon on the Arkansas River, 120 miles to the east. (No cavalry was available at nearby Fort Garland; manpower requirements for the Civil War, then raging in the East, had severely depleted all western military garrisons.)

Hiram Vasquez volunteered for the ride. That night, armed with a gun and a knife, clad in soft moccasins to muffle his footsteps, he slipped over the wall. He was familiar with the myriad trails leading east out of the Cuchara Valley onto the prairie, and utilizing all the skills he had learned during his Shoshone captivity, he moved swiftly and silently through the bush. Downstream on the Cuchara he found a corral with a few mules, and selecting a tough little nut-brown one he took off to the northeast, riding without pause toward the Arkansas River, where he arrived at mid-morning. Ravenous with hunger, he munched on jerky and hardtack while the mule chewed grass and drank from the river. Then he took off again, reaching Fort Lyons less than twenty-four hours after leaving his besieged comrades.

The commandant of the fort sent a detail of twenty cavalrymen, with Hiram in the lead, back to the Cuchara Valley. John Francisco had already convinced the Utes to depart, and when the detachment arrived the men were back at work, hammering and sawing.

El Grandote

El Grandote, a Tarahumara Indian from deep in Mexico, came to the Wahatoya with his brother-in-law to look for gold, leaving behind Nana, his beautiful wife, and their unborn child. One night he dreamed he saw Nana asleep, but when he looked closer he realized she was dead. Deeply disturbed, he returned to Mexico with his brother-in-law. When they arrived they found that not only Nana had been murdered but her father as well. In his grief, Grandote vowed he would be forever true to the memory of Nana and their unborn child.

While in Mexico, Grandote had another dream. In it the gods told him he must return to the Wahatoyas, for there he would find his beloved Nana.

So Grandote went back to the twin peaks and lay down to sleep at the mouth of a place called the Cave of the Gods. Nana came to him in his sleep, holding their infant son in her arms. Together they strolled, night after night, along the banks of the rippling streams and placid lakes of the Wahatoyas.

The gods then told him to go back to Mexico and bring all his people to the Wahatoyas. Grandote did so, and for years they lived in peace at the foot of the mountains. But then the white man came and made slaves of Grandote's people. Grandote prayed for help, and the gods responded by sending a rock slide roaring down the mountain, which buried the village and everyone in it. Only Grandote survived. He still walks the wild gorges of the twin mountains with his beloved wife and son.

5
Bear Dance

I was hesitant at first, standing in the opening of the cedar brush arbor until someone told me I should stand to the side and not block the view of the dancers. So I stood to the side with several other Indians and Anglos and looked inside, listening to the raspy sound of the *moraches* and the thunking of the ceremonial drum. It was early afternoon, bright and hot on the Southern Ute Reservation in southwest Colorado on the outskirts of the town of Ignacio. Outside the brush circle vendors peddled hamburgers, soft drinks, tacos, a variety of arts and crafts. Inside the circle two lines had formed, men on one side, women on the other; together, like a mirror image, locked in the rhythm of a two-step shuffle, they swayed back and forth.

It was Bear Dance time on the Southern Ute Reservation, home of the Capote and Muache bands. The origin of this ancient dance, oldest of all Ute ceremonies, is misty and vague. Two brothers were out hunting in the mountains when they grew tired and lay down to rest. A bear suddenly appeared, swaying and dipping in front of a tree, growling and clawing at the bark with its talons. One of the brothers went hunting while the other continued to observe the bear. The bear taught this brother how to do the dance and what to sing. Then he told the brother to return to his people and teach them what he had just learned.

Traditionally, the Bear Dance helped people release their tensions, built up during the long dreary months of the Rocky Mountain winter. As they entered the cedar circle, men and women wore plumes in their hair, which at the end of the fourth and final day of dancing they left on a cedar tree planted at the east entrance of the circle. According to the Utes, leaving the

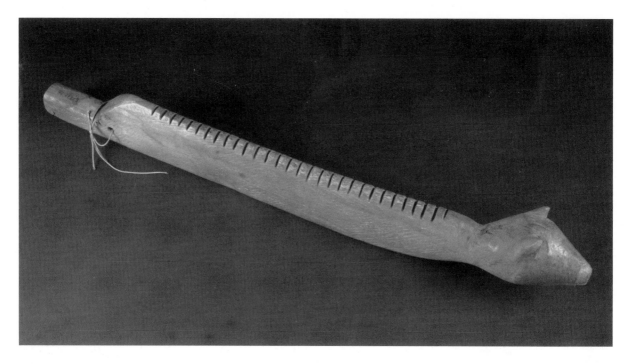

Morache, rasper, or bear growler. Courtesy, Colorado Historical Society.

plumes on the tree was akin to leaving your troubles behind and starting your life anew.

I stood at the opening to the circle for so long I began to feel like a wall-flower at a high-school mixer. One of the singers called to those of us lurking at the entrance to enter. "You're all welcome," he said. "You don't got to be Indian to have a good time. Check your inhibitions, and come on down!"

There were maybe a dozen people dancing inside the circle. The musicians consisted of eight raspers and one singer engaged in pumping out a sluggy, sawing rhythm—wonga-wonga-wonga—a deep chuffing sound like a bear waddling along a mountain trail looking for something to eat. The women who weren't dancing sat on the south arc of the circle to the right of the singer-raspers-drummers; the men sat on the west to their left in hard metal chairs. Okay, I thought. Okay now . . . and stepped through the opening. I pulled a sprig off the branch of one of the cedars near the opening, mashed it with my fingers, and rubbed the fragrance on my face and neck. I followed the inside arc of the arbor around to the chairs where the men sat. There were a few old guys, a sprinkling of youngsters, two or three middle-agers like myself. There was one other white guy, a tall, lanky redhead dressed in fancy boots, Levis, and a buckskin vest.

It was hot in the circle under the May sun, and the elders who'd come to watch sat under umbrellas and colorful parasols, stirring the air in front of their faces with straw fans. Boys wearing ball caps on backward and sloppy T-shirts sat in the audience near the elders, flipping yo-yos and chewing gum. The grass at the center of the spacious arena had been trampled by generations of dancing feet.

The music started up again—rat-cha-cha-cha, rat-cha-cha-cha, rat-cha-cha-cha—a low, throaty, guttural sound made by the raspers grinding deer bones along a notched stick. The sound seemed to enter my body through my abdomen, a gutty, visceral sensation that made me want to growl in response. The tips of the rasps rested on a wooden resonator covered with rawhide. Traditionally, the sound was designed to rumble through the earth and wake up the bears and the land after the long winter's sleep. The sound also signaled that it was time for members of the tribe to visit relatives, play games, mourn the departed, and bid welcome to new members of the tribe.

Petroglyph of deer incised by forerunners of the Utes, Comanche National Grasslands.

No one really knows where the Utes came from or how long they've lived in Colorado. The oral history of the tribe mentions few migration legends. The Utes say they've been where they are today for as long as they can remember. Anthropologists, who usually have a different idea than what Indians say in their oral traditions, offer little concrete evidence to the contrary.

Forerunners of the present-day Utes probably appeared in the Colorado region many hundreds of years ago. Archaeological evidence is scanty, but at some point the Utes drifted up to the mountains; their numbers were few, and they were confronted on all sides by enemies. Gradually, over a long period of trial and error, they adapted to the rugged highlands. Starvation

Abstract designs chipped by forerunners of the Utes, Apishapa Canyon.

was a chronic threat; sufficient food had to be stored away before the first big snow to last until spring.

By the 1650s the Utes had acquired enough horses from the Spanish to transform themselves into a nomadic culture. Twice a year they sallied forth from their mountain lairs to hunt buffalo down on the plains, which improved their diet and extended their influence over areas once dominated by their competitors—the Arapaho, Comanche, Kiowa, Pawnee, and Cheyenne. Dark and diminutive, reclusive and shy, they remained preeminently a mountain people. Their name for themselves was "Blue Sky People." They were superb defensive fighters, and they always knew that no matter what kind of scrape they got into they could melt back into the protective cover of the mountains.

Eventually two bands, the Muache and Capote, settled in southern Colorado. The Muache located in the San Luis Valley, the Sangre de Cristos, and the Spanish Peaks. The Spanish Peaks band probably never numbered more than a thousand people; by 1870 that number had been reduced to fewer than five hundred. A decade later they were confined with the Capote band on a narrow strip of land in the southwest corner of Colorado under the watchful eye of the U.S. military and religious missionaries.

Gradually during that first day, I learned the rules governing the behavior of the dancers: you mustn't dance with a relative, you mustn't look your partner in the face, you must always dance when asked.

Women initiate the dance. That afternoon, eyes averted, three or four stepped over, wearing fringed shawls around their shoulders. Casually, quietly, with supreme nonchalance, they approached within a few feet of where we sat. Just when I thought I'd been passed by, one of them flicked the tip of her shawl at me. Following my instructions, I waited a few moments before getting to my feet and joining her in the center of the circle. (It's considered undignified to display too much enthusiasm.)

There were a dozen of us, six men and six women, in two facing lines. Some of the women wore lots of silver and turquoise; others, including my partner, wore colorful full-length skirts, embroidered blouses pinned at the throat with beaded brooches, silk shawls fringed with soft tassels, and beaded moccasins that rose to mid-calf. The dance marshal, traditionally known as the cat man—an old guy sporting yellow kid gloves, an eagle feather sticking from his straw hat—waved a long curved stick to make sure we were all lined up properly. I took the hands of the men on either side, and as the music began we stepped forward and back with an awkward, tentative step that proved surprisingly aerobic. The dance was deceptively simple, a forward-dipping left-foot motion followed by the same motion executed in reverse. Two lines, male and female, each line holding hands, rocked back and forth with a step, half-step motion to the gnawing, grating, grinding rasp of the *moraches*. I don't know how long the dance lasted, maybe a few minutes, but when I sat down I was breathing hard. The musicians rested awhile, then started up again. Another woman flicked the tip of her shawl

Junior Miss Southern Ute at Bear Dance powwow, held same time as Bear Dance.

at me, and I got to my feet and headed for the center of the circle. This time we were joined by two male dancers about my age wearing Stetsons and beaded gauntlets, queues of glossy black hair dangling down their backs, who added a note of style and class to the male contingent.

I sat out the next dance and watched the newcomers, who obviously knew what they were doing. They placed their hands on their partners' waists, and with the females steadying themselves, each with a hand on the man's left shoulder, the two couples swept like antelopes to the edge of the arbor, the women dancing backward in long gliding steps. Then, with the men in reverse, they returned to the center with a light skipping stride reminiscent of a Spanish fandango.

I heard a meadowlark whistle somewhere outside the arbor. The musicians poked fun at the cat man, who looked sternly at a quartet of teenagers lining up awkwardly for the next dance. A murmur of good-natured laughter rippled around the interior of the circle. Then the growly ratch of the raspers started up again, and the teenagers took off, bounding with athletic grace to the edge of the arbor. The cat man nodded in approval. The musicians bore down on their instruments. The sun felt warm and soothing on my back and shoulders. The sweet aroma of hot cedar filled my nostrils. In a little while another woman approached and flicked the tip of her shawl at me.

The Valley of the Rising Sun

In the upper valley of Santa Clara Creek, at a spot covered with delicate ferns forming a soft carpet, the Indians built their altars to the Sun God. They worshiped here during the summer solstice. There was no rancor or discord, and people of different backgrounds were free to come and go without fear of being harmed.

One day dark clouds gathered over Huajatolla, and warlike invaders swarmed down from the north. The peaceful residents were overwhelmed and slaughtered.

The wanton attack angered the gods of Huajatolla. The Rain God refused to release any water. The Sun God glared down at the interlopers. The land became parched and dry. The trees withered and lost their needles and leaves.

Legend says the twin mountain erupted with geysers of fire and boiling mud—not exactly a volcano, with hot lava pouring down the slopes, but more like a self-contained eruption. Magma bubbling to the surface remained sealed under a layer of earth, never really cracking into the air. It was as if the gods were so upset at what had happened to the paradise they had helped to create that they couldn't decide whether to destroy it or make everyone suffer for a while.

6
More About Bears

Floyd Chavez is a solid, heavyset man in his mid-seventies. He walks with a stately waddle on a pair of severely bowed legs, seemingly in no hurry to get where he wants to go. His fleshy face looks as solemn as an Olmec mask until he smiles, when it brightens with a playful glow. I met him at his house outside the village of Weston on the south slope of the Spanish Peaks. Floyd owns a generous spread of prime land that rolls back from the banks of the Purgatoire River, through the foothills, to the tree-covered ridgelines at the top of the valley. In summer he grazes about a hundred and fifty cattle in the pine-clad hills behind his white stucco house with the blue metal roof. One day in mid-July he took me up in his Ford pickup to look around. We passed through a series of bright yellow gates ("Yellow is my favorite color," he says unabashedly) in the company of two feisty sheepdogs named Bandito and Benny Boy. A Mexican worker from Chihuahua named Manuel, a powerfully built man in his late thirties wearing jeans, dark glasses, and black T-shirt, came along with us.

We bounced over a rough track that led up and up, swaying like rag dolls in the front seat of the battered pickup. Manuel followed on a noisy four-wheeler. At each fence he swung off and opened the gate, never quite fast enough for Floyd, who grumped at him in a mix of "Spanglish." The two sheep dogs held on as best they could in the truck bed, but the going was so rough they lost their footing and rolled from side to side.

The day was beautiful, sunlit and mild, the sky fleeced with a few stringy clouds. A light breeze blew, stirring the bushy tips of the ponderosas and spruce. We passed several cattle clustered around a foul-looking water hole. Periodically, we stopped and watched Manuel pull a salt block off the

Floyd Chavez with Bandito and Benny Boy.

back of the pickup and set it up in an exposed place. Taut veins stretched like corded string the length of his muscular arms. At one point we passed a methane gas sink marked by tubes and pipes, which Floyd had leased to a prospector. "I've about had it with them folks," he growled. "This whole mountain's fulla gas, and they can't find any. I bet if I lit a cigarette I'd make a strike quicker'n they could."

As we rattled along, Floyd told a story about Manuel. Manuel was scared of bears. He'd had a few encounters down in Chihuahua and several up here. Last year he was working on a house at a religious retreat just off Highway 12, a mile or two from Floyd's house, when a black bear came out of the trees and snatched his lunch cooler. Manuel was up on the frame of the house and looked on helplessly as the bear banged the cooler against a tree trying to get at his lunch. "Manuel is as scared of bears as any Mexican I ever seen," Floyd gasped, tears flooding his dark brown eyes. "So what could he do? He stayed up on that frame nearly all afternoon while that silly bear whacked the cooler against any hard surface he could find. Finally, he threw the cooler away and disappeared into the trees. You shoulda seen Manuel's face when he told me the story. Oh, my!"

"Are there lots of bears up here?" I asked.

"Yes indeed. These hills are fulla bears. Last fall we shot one that weighed close to 600 pounds. It'd been prowling around my barn down below, and I was afraid for the dogs. So I let some hunters on the property, and they cornered it within a few hours. It was really big. One of the biggest I seen in all my years."

We bounced along in the truck, arms braced to keep from knocking our heads against the ceiling. The vanilla smell of sun-drenched ponderosa trunks seeped through the open windows. We stopped to open more gates and put out more salt blocks. "Time was," Floyd sighed, "when we didn't need keys or locks. We just shut the gate and people respected that."

It looked fairly dry and tindery where we were, although Floyd claimed they'd had plenty of rain. "That's the way it is in this piney country," he remarked. "Them mats of needles just suck the moisture right out of the ground."

"That and the rocks," I offered, pointing at an exposed formation of sandy red rock rising out of the crown of a hill.

"That rock caught the eye of a spiritual fellow a few years ago. He offered me a big price for a few acres of hilltop right here so he could build a little shack and have access to the rock. He claimed it was some kind of holy site."

"Was he Indian?"

"No. He was white. He wore a cross around his neck, an eagle feather in his hair, and carried a boxful of crystals." A faint smile curled the corners of his mouth. "Covering all his bases, I guess."

We reached the top of the ridge, and Floyd braked the pickup to a halt. We swung out of the cab and sauntered over to an exposed ledge, Floyd rolling on his bowed legs like a sailor across the deck of a pitching ship.

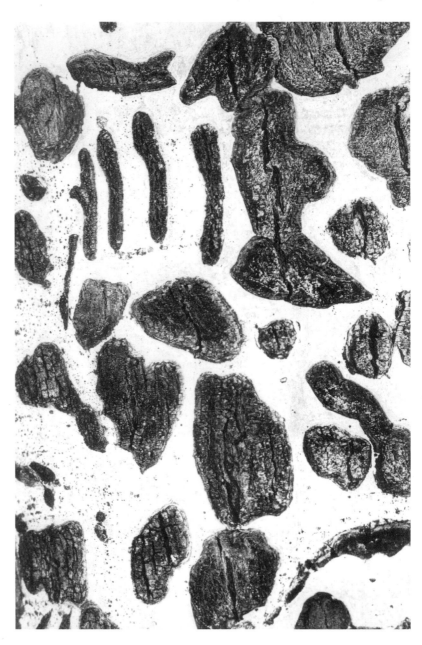

Bear claw marks, aspen tree.

The ledge offered a scenic view of the Purgatoire Valley. Foamy suds dappled the brown surface of the swift-flowing river as it charged down toward the flats. The fields next to the river brimmed with silky grass. A few orchards and cultivated plots were visible, but the land was mainly pasturage. To the northwest shone the red roof of the new San Ysidro Church, beyond that the abandoned buildings of the former Allen coal mine.

We settled on the ledge a few feet from a sheer drop that fell away a hundred feet or more to the dark ripply cover of a conifer forest. Bandito

San Ysidro Church outside Weston.

and Benny Boy snuffed through the brush, fussing and growling. Manuel squat nearby, not too close, and smoked a cigarette.

Floyd had been raised in this same valley. His great-grandfather had homesteaded here in the 1860s, one of the first Hispanic pioneers to settle in the region. "He got mixed up in the Stonewall War back in the 1880s," said Floyd. "The people who ran the big Maxwell Land Grant tried to throw the homesteaders off their land. They had a shoot-out up in Stonewall where several people got killed. I remember hearing them stories as a boy. Seems like the history of the Spanish Peaks usually involves some kind of shooting."

"How about the big coal strike?"

"Oh sure, that too. That was before my time, but I remember hearing about it from my grandfather."

"Did you ever work in the mines?"

A snort of laughter lit up Floyd's fleshy face. "Not me, not me. We've had mine disasters around here, more than you can count, where the bodies were never recovered. I got too much of a yellow streak down my back to live my life like a gopher."

He took off his white straw cowboy hat and swept a pudgy hand through his thin gray hair. "When I got out of the navy in 1946, my father and grandfather cosigned for a little farm down below. I was lucky. I had help. They knew all the bankers in Trinidad. But I guess I ran it okay, 'cause within ten years I paid it off and added a few new acres."

"Where did you serve?"

"I was in the navy. South Pacific. I wanted to go in the air force, but I was too young and my parents wouldn't sign for me. I had an uncle who'd been in World War I, and he told me to go in the navy where they had the best food. I did, and he was right. I went in in 1942 at age seventeen. Served as a motor machinist's mate on a destroyer escort. I was at Saipan, Leyte Gulf, Iwo Jima, and Okinawa. At Iwo I watched the marines raise the flag on Suribachi. They had to do it twice, once for themselves, once for the photographers. At Okinawa we had the stuffing kicked out of us by them kamikazes. You can't image how awful that was. They threw everything they could at us, day and night. We took a hell of a beating. I was sitting with a buddy in an open gun turret when a Jap Zero slammed into the bridge. I flew up, I flew down. Somewhere I hit my head and lost consciousness. The ship caught fire, but we stayed onboard and put it out."

"So after the war you came back to where you grew up?"

"I never lived in a city in my life. I been to enough of them in the navy to know that's not where I want to be. I like having my own private place with these woods and hills and that river down there. I want to be able to lie down on a bed of pine needles and not be afraid of getting run over."

He removed his hat and wiped his forehead with a polka-dot bandanna. Benny Boy sniffed at his feet, then went romping off to find Bandito. Manuel had disappeared between the trees. Floyd was full of stories, and he no sooner finished one then he launched into another. Pain registered visibly on his face as he recounted how his son had been shot trying to mediate a quarrel between two friends. One of them pulled a pistol and it went off, and the bullet hit his son in the chest, killing him instantly.

There was nothing I could say to console him. Sometimes you can only listen to so much, and then the weight of what you hear acts like a wedge, creating an unbridgeable gap between you and the speaker.

"Where'd that damn guy go?" Floyd grumbled. His face looked heavy and sad. As if on cue, Manuel stepped into the clearing where the pickup was parked. He didn't glance our way. Instead, he lit a cigarette and slowly pulled on his leather gloves and made a clicking noise between his teeth to the dogs, who jumped in the back of the pickup.

As we jolted over the uneven ground, swerving to miss the occasional rock, keys and ammo shells scattered on top of the dash clicking like marble beads, Floyd told another story. "I musta been about fourteen, I guess. I was out with a buddy I called the Professor. He was a good guy, not real bright, but he was my best friend, and instead of calling him Stupid, we called him the Professor. We knew where this animal was hibernating. It was the dead of winter, and we thought we'd see if we couldn't wake it up. We thought it was a badger, though neither the Professor or me had seen it actually go into the hole. But we found it anyway, and being kids I guess we were bored. It was January, and it was cold like it gets here, with lots of snow. Well, we found the hole, and when we looked in we could see this big furry thing curled up asleep. So like a pair of nuts, we decided to pull it out by the back legs and see what kind of animal it really was. Well, we both knelt down in front of the hole like a pair of choirboys praying on their knees. I had a rusty single-shot .22 rifle, and when we heard it growl I looked at the Professor and he looked at me, and I brought the rifle up to my shoulder, and when I heard it growl again and saw the flash of its teeth I pulled the trigger. The bullet went right into its brain, and it died right there, and we both leaned into the hole and pulled it out, and it was a bear! Well, I couldn't believe it, and neither could the Professor. Now we had this bear on our hands, and it was pretty big, and we had no idea what to do with it.

"I'd always been attracted to bears. I don't know exactly why, but I was about to find out. We made a kind of stretcher out of sticks and carried him back to my father's barn. We got him in the barn and strung him up by the hind feet and took his guts out and let the blood drip on the ground. Then we skinned him, and with most of the fat off he looked like a human being. It spooked us to see limbs and muscles and an anatomy that looked so much like our own. The Professor got pretty bug-eyed about it, and so did I. I didn't want to keep the bear in the barn. One time my dad tried to bring a dead bear in the house, and my mother had a fit. 'Not here,' she kept saying. 'You aren't bringing that animal in here. It belongs outside.'

"So we went in the dead of night to a family by the name of Silva. I knew they'd take the bear. They were a big family, with lots of kids and no money to speak of, and they'd pretty much eat anything. So in the middle of the night, after we'd finished skinning the bear, we hauled it to their house and knocked on the door. 'Who are you? What'd you want?' old man Silva hissed through the crack in the door.

"I guess it was pretty late, and we could've been outlaws for all he knew. 'Well Mr. Silva,' I said, 'it's Floyd Chavez and the Professor, and we shot this bear and I can't leave it hanging in my dad's barn, and we thought you maybe might be able to use it.'

"Well, he come out of that house in his long underwear, hair flying. 'Where is it?' he whispered. 'Where do you have it?'

"'Right here, Mr. Silva,' I said, and we picked the naked bear up on its bed of sticks so he could see it by the light of his kerosene lamp. A big grin split his face, and he stepped back and held the door open for us, the front door, mind you. 'Bring it on in, boys,' he said. He had a smile on his face as wide as Christmas morning. 'Put it right there on the table.'"

"*Oso*! *Oso*!"

Manuel was riding in the four-wheeler on our left. We had just crossed a clearing and were about to enter the trees on the other side when he saw the bear and cried out. Floyd braked the pickup to an abrupt halt. "What's he crying about," he started to say when we both saw it: a huge, frowzy, cinnamon-colored bear with a whitish chest, dark snout, pointy ears, and wide, taloned paws, standing in front of a grove of gambel oaks about 40 feet in front of us. I pulled my binoculars out of my shirt pocket, but I was so rattled I put the wrong end to my eyes, and instead of being magnified the bear shrank to the size of a plastic toy. A low grunt issued from Floyd's throat. I heard my own breath rasping between my teeth. Manuel stood straight up on the sideboards of the four-wheeler and pointed at the creature with both hands. His mouth and jaw flapped like a marionette's, but no sound came forth; he continued to stand there on the vehicle, gesturing and working his jaw up and down. Bandito and Benny Boy were eerily quiet. I half expected them to leap out of the truck and challenge the bear, but they remained in back, whimpering and working their tails. I flipped the binoculars over and, after a few wavering attempts, sighted in on the bear, which continued to stand between the pines and the gambel oaks and regard us with no apparent urgency.

I had never been this close to a wild bear before, and I was astounded at how placid and calm it appeared, as if coming upon a party of humans rattling about in a pair of vehicles was no big deal. "Ah, ah," I heard myself gasp, and then the bear dropped on all fours and padded a few steps to its left, then back to the right. Unlike other animals who spook at the presence of a human, the bear was in control of the situation; as long as it wanted to look, we would do likewise. No one had a gun, and the dogs were sticking to the truck; we could all maintain a kind of tenuous threshold between the two worlds—watchful, cautious, wary—whereby we could regard one another for what seemed an endless length of time but that probably lasted no more than a minute. "*O-so-oo,*" I heard Manuel mutter again, this time in a whisper, at which the bear, for whatever reason, shuffled toward the trees on its right. It didn't turn and flee. It made no movement in haste or panic. It seemed to back up, lean to the right, then slip unobtrusively between the trees, its reddish-brown coloration blending smoothly with the rusty hues of the ponderosa trunks. One moment it was there, a huge, hulking, blowzy presence; the next it was gone.

Floyd rapped his right thumb against the steering wheel and rocked his heavy body back and forth. "How about that?" he wheezed. "How about that?"

The Gorge of Strange Sounds

There's a gorge that girdles the base of the Spanish Peaks that's filled with wild animals—bears, deer, cougar, wild turkeys, and porcupines. It's here, at certain times of the day and night, that the strange, sacred song of the majestic double mountain can be heard. Sometimes the song resonates like the chime of bells, sometimes it rumbles like the deep tones of an organ, commencing with a patter of soft, smooth notes and rising to a piercing crescendo.

It's said that the gods once dwelt in this gorge and that today it is haunted by their spirits.

7
La Veta 2

The dirt streets had already been wet down when I arrived a little before nine that morning. At the ball diamond on the outskirts of town a Little League game was in progress, attended by puffy-eyed parents clutching plastic coffee mugs who whooped it up as best they could when somebody scored or made a play. I eased the car into the last parking spot on Main in front of Charlie's General Store. Inside the quaint emporium with its creaky floor and old-time soda fountain, I purchased a cup of coffee and my favorite roadie breakfast food, a synthetically flavored apple turnover with a gluey golden center encrusted with splots of stale white sugar. Outside, on a bench in front of the Covered Wagon across the street, I sat down and proceeded to enjoy this hearty repast. There was a barbecue in La Veta City Park starting at noon, but that was hours away, and I needed a cheap snack to kick myself awake for the morning festivities. The shade under the *portales* spanning the width of the sidewalk retained a measure of nocturnal coolness. It was only nine-thirty, but out in the street the sun blazed fiercely. The sandstone facades of the buildings across the street shone with a faint pink glow. An American flag and a Colorado state flag dangled from twin poles on either side of the entrance to Charlie's. On the window next to the door someone had painted a huge pop-art ice cream cone in luminous detail, down to the tiny cross-hatching on the stubby yellow cone.

On the next bench under the refreshing shade sat a roundish elderly fellow with a flushed pink complexion, gripping a slim wooden cane banded with bright colors. Around his neck he wore a bandanna bearing the stars and stripes of the American flag. July Fourth was three days off, but La Veta was celebrating early—a parade, scheduled to start at eleven A.M., followed by a barbecue and live music by a Dixieland band.

"Big day today," the old guy declared.

"Yep. So I've heard."

"Town turns out in full force for this one."

"Looks like it attracts a few outsiders as well."

"Oh them." He waved a pudgy hand toward a smart-looking couple standing in the middle of the street shielding their eyes with their hands, as if trying to make up their minds about something. "You can always tell by how they dress. Golf shirts, straw hats, two-toned shoes."

"Looks like they carry water bottles to boot," I added.

"That, too," the man agreed. He tapped the tip of his cane against the sidewalk. "We got pretty good water around here, right from the spigot. Comes out of the Cuchara, which flows right off the peaks. I drank it all my life and never got sick."

"You from these parts?"

"Born and raised and lived my entire life in this exact place."

He dabbed his lips with a corner of his patriotic bandanna. His pink face resembled a hairless tennis ball. His age was indecipherable—fifty? Seventy?

"'Cept for four years on a guided-missile cruiser in the navy."

"What was that like?"

"Enlightening. Yes, that's how I'd characterize it."

"In what ways?"

"Met a lot of different people. Learned a lot of interesting things. Operated some pretty special machinery."

"Missiles?"

"Uh-hum."

"So why'd you come back here? After that experience you could've lived anywhere you wanted."

"I lived in Cal'fornia for two years but didn't much like it. Too many people. Too many goldanged cars. Besides, what other place you know of has two of the prettiest mountains in the world settin' right outside your front door?"

"That's true."

"There's nothing quite like them sisters. I see 'em as two sisters, one in front of the other, one leading the other, like ships with triangular sails beating to windward against a bad-weather coast."

"Somebody whose family has lived around here for at least three generations told me they were yin and yang, male and female. Symbolic of the polar opposites in life."

The man squinted narrowly my direction, a faint trace of suspicion darkening his face. In the shadow cast by the *portales* his eyes seemed to draw back deep into his skull until they practically disappeared. "I bet I know who tole you that!" he whispered with alarming intensity.

"I'm not telling."

"'Course not. No gentleman ever would. However, I think that person is wrong. Them peaks're both women. Sisters, maybe. Or maybe mother and daughter. Sometimes in the moonlight I think they're mother and daughter, sailing in tandem through the universe. Whatever, they're my touchstones, my totems. I'll never live any place other than here."

"People have told me stories about UFO activities around these peaks." I held my breath, but what the hell, it was the Fourth of July (or close to it), and I wanted to keep this guy talking.

His eyes reappeared in his forehead, round and glaucous, slightly startled, like the eyes of a surfacing fish. A snort escaped his lips. He banged the tip of the banded cane against the sidewalk between his feet. "Don't get me started, mister," he growled. "I could tell you stories that'd curl your hair."

Before the parade I wandered around La Veta City Park, inspecting the booths, watching a bunch of men fire up their grills and barbecue ovens with mesquite sticks. A bumper sticker pasted on the outside of an open lid read: "I Brake for Animals. I Eat Them and Wear Their Skins."

The atmosphere was jovial. Families were unfolding chairs and setting up picnic tables in the generous shade of the trees. People greeted one another with hugs, high fives, and vigorous handshakes. The air was filled with a blend of accents—slurry Texas drawls, clipped mountain talk, reticent enthusiasm from social types wearing pressed khaki shorts and banlon shirts with country club logos. Several locals wandered around in Uncle Sam outfits, complete with buckled shoes and candy-striped top hats. Women wore festival dresses with long flowing skirts and frilly lace bodices. Children danced in circles, squealing with delight, followed by yapping dogs.

Promptly at eleven the parade began, led by a quintet of U.S. Cavalry reenactors dressed in blue wool uniforms and carrying facsimile Sharps carbines. Like most reenactors they were completely into their thing and passed the spot on the curb where I stood with fierce expressions, so contrary to the prevailing mood of hilarity and good fun. Following these came a contingent of doughty Shriners on foot, bearing a curious display of flags—United States, Mexico, Canada, Colorado, and Panama—the last an odd choice, more appropriate for a yacht marina than a land-locked town in south-central Colorado. The Huerfano County 4-H queen, a nubile beauty, trailed the Shriners mounted on a reddish-colored stallion, accompanied by a trio of equally fetching young ladies wearing tight Levis, beaded denim shirts, and broad-brimmed cowboy hats. A summer reading library float followed the queen and her consort, packed with kids propelling bits of candy at the spectators on both sides of the street with paddlelike swats from the backs of their books. A 1955 two-tone, two-door Chevy Belair bearing a banner with a man's name and the county office he was running for rumbled by, followed by a quartet of small children dressed in matching outfits, mounted on tall prancing horses.

The sun radiated a fierce glare, but it was cool under the spreading locust trees that lined Charlie's side of the street. A man in a wheelbarrow

Boy dressed as nineteenth-century soldier, Fourth of July.

pulled by a goat in a Denver Broncos cap trotted past, followed by four Shetland ponies marching abreast under the stern commands of a middle-aged woman whose jeans were perhaps two sizes too small for her ample hips and posterior. There was an early 1900s vintage automobile driven by a man in a long white duster with yellow-tinted goggles. Next to him sat an exquisite old lady with delicate well-bred features, clad in a flowing satin dress that had to be uncomfortable in this heat. A parasol shielded her face from the sun; every few seconds her right hand floated off her lap and dipped in regal fashion to the crowd, which hooted in appreciation.

More politicians paraded by, some in pickups, some on floats, some in cars. They waved and honked and pointed at their banners. A candidate working the crowd on foot paused to shake my hand and jam a pamphlet into my shirt pocket. "Appreciate your vote!" he boomed, moving on to the next constituent. Something tugged at my knee. A little girl with her hair tied in a topknot with a pretty bow pointed at the front of her T-shirt. "Vote for My Daddy," it said, which she parroted in a puny voice barely audible over the hoopla. I touched her cheek, to which she flashed an automatic smile and moved on to catch up with her energetic father.

An ancient McCormick-Deering tractor rattled past, driven by a geezer in coveralls, straw hat, and scruffy beard who looked as if he had emerged from a time capsule. A sleek black 1936 convertible Ford roadster puttered by bearing a pair of blades in seersucker suits and straw boaters, accompanied by two women dressed as flappers with bobbed hair and cadaverous makeup. A pair of noisy, whistling ambulances brought up the rear, accompanied by a fire truck that blasted its air horn, much to the delight of the kids and the consternation of two old people perched in wheelchairs, who grimaced and tried to cover their ear holes with the tips of their speckled fingers.

The entire procession ran the length of Main Street from south to north, then made a wide looping turn through a filling station and started back. The effect the second time wasn't as gratifying as the first, though the paraders tried to compensate for the lack of surprise by behaving even more boisterously. The politicians whooped and clasped their hands and waved them over their heads. A saucy lass in a skimpy bikini stood up from a tractor seat to reveal the full delights of her curvaceous figure. Fistfuls of candy whirled through the air like buckshot. Children on the curbs darted into the street to retrieve as much as they could, sparking groans of alarm from their supervising adults.

Then as now, Fourth of July was a major celebration for the people of La Veta. Back in 1881 the day began with the firing of a fifty-gun salute. Promptly at ten A.M. the procession formed on the commons fronting the La Veta Hotel (La Veta Town Park today). Thirty-five mummers, known as "calithumpians," masked and decked out in fantastical costumes, followed the musicians, a five-piece Italian band imported from Pueblo. Next in line came the decorated carriages packed with women and children, wearing their Sunday finery and singing patriotic songs. Aside from the calithumpians, the main attraction was a large wagon festooned with evergreens, pulled by four horses and carrying thirty-eight boys and girls, each representing a state in the Union. Miss Jessie Burch, buxom and comely, sheathed in a form-fitting white dress—the incarnation of virginal purity and promise— stood on a platform in the center of the float, the very image of the Goddess of Liberty. Following the float came a company of local men riding burros and dressed as 1859 Pikes Peak prospectors. Caught up in the swell of emotion, spectators fell in behind the prospectors, and the entire cavalcade tromped through the streets, singing and shouting and waving banners.

Devil's Stairsteps

Long ago, when the earth was new, the Devil was allowed out of his fiery home to have a look at the world. He chose the Cuchara Valley as the place to make his appearance. He climbed up the steps of the tall dike and sat down in the cleft between the two peaks. He liked what he saw and plotted how to take control of it all. God soon learned of his scheme, and loving the beauty of the valley and mountains He forbade the Devil to enter the region again. But the Devil's Stairsteps still stand. And the Devil found other places in the world to make mischief.

8
The Dividing Line

Tom Doerk walks up the side of the mountain like he's strolling along a canopied boardwalk on the outskirts of a fashionable Swiss spa. He carries two packs, mine and his, and he walks with a slight swing of the arms, chatting animatedly about this and that. It's a cool, pleasant late-spring morning on the west edge of the Spanish Peaks. Sunlight gleams in soft yellow bands through the narrow slots between the congested trees—aspen, ponderosa, Engelmann spruce, limber pine. Now and then I look up from the drudgerous labor of putting one foot in front of the other. The trail is soggy in spots from melting snowpacks, and the footing is tricky. Up and up I toil, huffing and puffing, thrusting the ponderous weight of my middle-aged body against the mantle of burdensome gravity. I feel like a worm boring through a vat of soggy treacle. Going uphill is not my favorite direction, and I take it at my accustomed turtle crawl, much to Tom's amusement. "Well, shake a leg there!" he yells down at me. But I literally can't go any faster. I can barrel downhill with surprising speed, but going up—oh God!—is always so painfully slow.

It's a steep climb from the Bear Lake parking lot through a dense, tangled forest littered with deadfall. Up and up we proceed, Tom way out front at times, then pausing to let me catch up. "The tortoise and the hare," I gasped at one point.

"Tortoise?" Tom grinned. "You're like some kind of armored pachyderm! Most glaciers make better time than you!"

"Can't help it," I puffed. "It's like an existential punishment, the accumulated weight of all my sins and shortcomings."

Off to the right we hear the sound of the Cuchara River, gushing and tumbling downhill, carrying the liquid runoff from this side of the watershed. Countless tiny rivulets trickle out from under grimy snowpacks, nosing their way downhill, merging with countless others, blending, folding, spilling into a common thread.

An hour later, much to Tom's amusement ("You turtles are hard on us gazelles!"), we arrived at a major fork in the trail. One trail branched west toward the summit of Mount Trinchera in the Culebra Range; the second angled south toward the Purgatoire campground 6 miles distant. Our destination lay along this route, so we continued up a ways, slogging through more snowy heaps sprinkled with fallen pine needles. Finally we arrived at a smooth, rounded place where the trail seemed to peak. Somewhere around here, Tom maintained, was the dividing line between two of the principal rivers of the Spanish Peaks region, the Cuchara and the Purgatoire—the former flowing north and east, the later south and east. The trail at this point skirted a pleasant sunlit field shaped in an elongated oval, edged with snowpacks, tufted with marsh marigolds and tightly folded plumelike growths of young skunk cabbage. There was also wild iris, the predominant iris of the West, found in moist meadows around 8,000 feet, once used in the treatment of syphilis. Tiny pines dotted the field, taking hold, recapitulating the endless struggle between open space and encroaching forest.

A gray jay whisked on fluffy wings from limb to limb around the periphery of the field, checking me out as I teetered upright near the center of its feeding ground, mired in boggy glop to my ankles. A flash of wings, and the bird glided from one downed limb to the next, scoping me at an oblique angle, quickly, furtively.

We had reached a watershed of sorts, the obvious indicator being the fact that we were no longer going up. Heaped with snow in the winter, the oval field felt bouncy under my boots; with each new step I sank deeper into the turf. The sun beamed pleasantly overhead; the forest enclosing us on all sides was littered with dead limbs and uprooted trees. The habitat here at the crown was moist and damp, the trees bedecked with lacy green moss. The forest floor was seamed and rumpled with decaying limbs and trunks, some so spongy and rotten my foot sank through them when I applied my weight.

We paused to examine a long, straight Engelmann spruce evidently uprooted by recent winds, lying on its side like a bowling pin, revealing a huge clumpy pedestal packed with rust-colored dirt and wiry roots. "A cross section of the forest right here in your face," Tom explained. "The sudden demise of this tree will help liberate the adjacent trees. Now, with space made suddenly available, more light will pour in, and the surrounding trees, which had struggled in the shadow of this lordly pine, will fill in the new gap."

"Location, location, location," I murmured.

Tom rolled his eyes and continued along the trail.

So this is what it's all about, I thought. Not the grandiose scenic effects, but the subtle stirrings of organic activity whose myriad replication leads to the larger linkups. Water, trickling water, meltwater, as if the mountain were bleeding from innumerable vents and pores. This goes on and on, not only within our purview but out of sight, repeated millions of times, each trickle both adding to the landscape and carrying something off, subtracting at the same time it replenishes. An incessant, inexorable process.

Back on the trail, a few yards along we come upon a sizable pool extending well into the trees on either side of the submerged path. We search the pool carefully, looking for telltale signs. The center portion looks glittery and quiescent, a smooth onyx surface reflecting the mass of trees surrounding it. The edges of the pool, however, appear ripply with some kind of gravity-induced animation. Hmm. Something going on here. I squat like a toad and let my eyes rove over the surface. Uh-huh. The water at the edge of the pool appears to trickle off north in the direction of the Cuchara River. Prowling the opposite end, Tom makes a similar discovery, water spilling south in minuscule drops, heading (eventually) for the Purgatoire. Of course, this isn't the only spot where the phenomenon occurs, but that doesn't matter. This is it—subtle, almost imperceptible, a microcosmic watershed that also doubles as a county line, spanning two river systems and two political enclaves (Huerfano and Las Animas Counties) as well.

As if in raucous affirmation, the wind suddenly tears through the tops of the trees with a swift rush. High winds have plagued this part of Colorado all spring, down on the flats as well, kicking up fires and clouds of dust from freshly plowed fields. The top of a blue spruce in Tom's yard was torn off by a mini-twister that danced through La Veta two weeks ago.

We start down a slight incline into the watershed of the North Fork of the Purgatoire, following the soggy trail, plowing through deep snowpacks. Midday sunlight, beaming overhead, refracts into countless slants and puddles, dappled by damp shadows in which a trace of winter's chill can still be felt. Then, a few minutes later, we come out from under the shadow of the trees onto a sun-drenched sweep of treeless slope threaded by a faint trail. The site, apparently, of a long-ago fire that blazed across the hillside extinguishing trees and understory, leaving a few dead boles and trunks, ash gray and wind-smoothed, sticking up at crazy angles. Bristlecone pines mark the edge of the ecotone. Short, squat trees, uniformly thick, with fibrous needles, sticky with fresh sap.

Out here in the open, the sun glimmers with a radiant sheen. A sky of pure cerulean sweeps overhead. A cool invigorating breeze flutters in from the west, down the slopes of the Culebra Range. Culebra, *snake* in Spanish, and now I understand why. A line of north-south peaks, packed shoulder to shoulder, presenting a slinky, undulating profile that walls off all possible views of the San Luis Valley to the west. Trinchera Peak, directly in front of us, reveals steep sides indented with deep hollow bowls gouged out by crunching glaciers.

The contrast of colors from this vantage point was startling. Shiny wedding-cake icing of the Culebra peaks, dark swatches of pine forest sweeping south along the valley of the Purgatoire, fading to chlorophyll

Culebra Range viewed
from western ramparts of
Spanish Peaks.

aspens at the lower levels. The visual tug was irresistible, the valley swoop-
ing south and east, the long line of shimmering trees, furrowed in their
deepest folds by the descending path of the North Fork of the Purgatoire.
My feet seemed to lift a little, buoyed by the wind, the splendid view, the
spectacle of a landscape that seemed in the act (on this flawless spring day)
of recharging itself with the bounty and vigor of its own inexhaustible
parts.

We left the trail and started directly upslope through the old fire area—
sticks, limbs, trunks, branches colored a smooth marmoreal gray, annealed
by fire and decades of wind and snow. Amid the ruck of broken limbs and
splintered trunks, a few pine seedlings have taken hold, a few aspen as well.
Up and up we toil, or rather I toil, for Tom springs ahead like a goat (he's
ten years younger than I) while I plod in his wake, one slow, careful step at
a time, pausing frequently, sucking cool mountain air deep into my grateful
lungs. Around me growths of gentian, bluebells, strawberries, and edel-
weiss. Tiny white butterflies gambol about my hands and legs like bits of
blown paper. I pass a flag tree, shorn of branches on its west side, and
finally mount to the top of the ridgeline. Tom lies sprawled against a fallen
log, clutching a water bottle, a bright smile spangling his thin, chiseled face.
"Welcome! I was going to send some stretcher bearers, but I see you made
it anyway!"

He waves his arm to the east. There, in majestic splendor, rise the Spanish Peaks, slick with snow at their summits. Ah. Good morning, friends. A half turn to the west and I face the sinuous Culebras with their gilded crowns and steep sides. Fulcrum, point of repose and promise, the spot where the peaks merge into the Culebra, each a product of separate geologic forces, nudging one another at right angles.

"Nice, isn't it?" Tom says with a relaxed smile.

A pair of crows, croaking loudly, sails overhead, rising on outspread wings that glisten like shiny metal in the midday sun.

Arapaho Princess Treasure

In the early 1800s a handsome Spaniard found a rich lode of gold in the foothills of the Spanish Peaks. As the mine grew bigger, he hired some Arapaho Indians to help him. The daughter of the chief was very beautiful, and the Spaniard fell in love with her. In due time they married and had a little girl.

When a band of Utes threatened to attack their camp, the Arapaho chief advised his son-in-law to leave as quickly as possible. The Spaniard loaded the gold on a burro train, but the Utes were close by, and he had to bury the gold in a place marked by a special rock with an iron shovel on top. In the confusion the Spaniard lost touch with his wife, and they were separated. Ten years later, when he returned to the peaks, he discovered that she had died. The news devastated him, and he lost all interest in the gold he had cached.

His daughter had survived and eventually grew up and married, but the Spaniard still grieved for his wife. On his deathbed he told his daughter and her husband where the gold was hidden. But he warned them that it was cursed and would bring only sorrow to anyone who tried to recover it.

The daughter and her husband never touched the hidden treasure. On her deathbed she revealed to her sons where they could find it under a rock with an old iron shovel marking the spot. The sons rushed to the site and searched everywhere but couldn't find it. A neighbor mentioned that the previous fall, while deer hunting, he had picked up an old shovel from one of the rocks and used it to clear away snow from his campsite. When asked if he could remember the rock on which he had found the shovel, the man shook his head. "All these rocks look the same," he shrugged.

The treasure still lies there for the taking.

9
Bent's Fort

It's easy to forget who you are at Bent's Fort. Time has a way of bending and warping, bringing the past to a point of convergence with the present. Perhaps it's the period detail, so punctiliously reproduced—the storerooms, living quarters, blacksmith shop, commissary. Perhaps it's the location, northeast of La Junta, Colorado, on the wide sweep of the plains close to the Arkansas River. Perhaps it's the structure itself, a low, squat, adobe redoubt, fastidiously reconstructed by the National Park Service to the size and scale of the original. Although it's not all that big, you can get lost in this place. You can imagine that it's 1840, and you're stopping over from the long haul along the Santa Fe Trail, and you're strolling one of the parapets on the roof of the compound, looking out upon miles of encampments spreading east and west along both sides of the Arkansas River. The smells are missing, the sounds, the animals, the extraordinary mix of cultures and races. French was once spoken here, English, Spanish, Portuguese, German, probably a dozen different Indian languages. From the early 1830s to about 1849, there was no place like Bent's Fort on the southwest plains. It combined a variety of functions—fort, trading post, entrepôt, oasis. It was a place where people of all backgrounds gathered to exchange gossip, argue politics, and trade raw material for manufactured goods.

Then as now, Bent's Fort served as a portal, a point of entry to the Spanish Peaks region. From the top of the circular tower at the northwest corner, the peaks are visible on a clear day, 80 miles away. Binoculars help, but I was able to distinguish their outline—shimmery, hazy, as if enveloped in a kind of terrestrial fluid—with the naked eye. I made this discovery one

Interior, Bent's Fort.

afternoon in late April and felt a tremor of excitement as I honed in on the fields of crusty white snow clinging to the upper slopes.

The peaks also served as a beacon for travelers on the mountain route of the Santa Fe Trail as they toiled southwest from Bent's Fort toward Raton Pass and the passage down into New Mexico. Day after day in bright sunlight, glowing in the luminous sheen of the moon, wreathed with streaky clouds at dawn and dusk, drenched by dark thunderheads, drawing the weary travelers closer to their destination.

It was beaver that attracted the first trappers to this part of Colorado in the 1820s and 1830s. They came from the east over the curve of the plains, following the sun and the sandy rivers that, west of the hundredth meridian, offered the only shade and water for their horses. They came via the Platte, way north in Nebraska, or the Smoky Hill through western Kansas, or the Arkansas and Red Rivers farther south in Kiowa and Comanche country. They had heard about the rich beaver streams in the Sangre de Cristos, and they were eager to tap into them. When they got to Taos, an isolated village nestled in a high valley in northern New Mexico, they outfitted themselves and slipped off without fanfare so as not to alert the Mexican authorities as to who they were and why they were there. They had to be wary of the Utes as well, people of the high slopes and valleys who welcomed whites if they had goods to trade but who objected if they planted corn, trapped animals, hunted buffalo, or appropriated any of the resources of this bountiful land for their personal use.

And so it went for the first three decades of the nineteenth century, with American trappers stepping lightly through the southern Rockies in search of beaver. Mexican officials, who succeeded their Spanish counterparts in 1821, proved equally touchy and intractable. Many a trapper spent time in jails in Santa Fe, Taos, and Chihuahua City for collecting "plews" in places where they clearly weren't welcome. But the markets were there, and any frontiersman worth his salt tried to finagle his way into the territory, begging, bribing, bluffing—whatever it took to cut a deal.

Between autumn of 1832 and October the following year, the bottom dropped out of the beaver market. Plews fell from $6 a pound to $3.50. The call from back East was for buffalo hides, which could be tanned and cut up to make tough leather straps to power the pulleys in the textile factories of New England. And so St. Louis–born William Bent and his older brother Charles, in partnership with an energetic Frenchman named Ceran St. Vrain, built a trading post on the north bank of the Arkansas River about 70 miles downstream from the mouth of Fountain Creek. (At that time the Arkansas River marked the boundary between the fledgling United States and the even more fledgling Republic of Mexico.) They then set about wooing the Plains tribes—Arapaho, Cheyenne, Kiowa, Comanche—into trading buffalo hides for the manufactured goods that arrived over the Santa Fe Trail by wagon train from the Missouri frontier.

The fort's location was selected with special care. It had to be close enough to the Rockies to attract trappers, close enough to the hunting grounds of the Plains tribes, close enough to the mountain branch of the Santa Fe Trail. Within a short time the fort, with its impressive battlements and palisades, was transformed into a cynosure, a haven, a crossroads. Indians came to trade and palaver. White folks came to find water, rest their animals, reprovision their supplies, escape from Indian attacks, read a book, and enjoy a meal served on real china. "Inside is a large space some ninety or a hundred feet square," wrote Susan Shelby Magoffin in 1846, one of the few females travelers to pass along the trail (quoted in Drumm, p. 60):

> All around this and next the wall are rooms, some twenty-five in
> number. They have dirt floors—which are sprinkled with water several
> times during the day to prevent dust. Standing in the center of some of
> them is a large wooden post as a firmer prop to the ceiling which is made
> of logs. Some of these rooms are occupied by boarders as bed chambers.
> One is a dining room—another a kitchen—a little store, a blacksmith's
> shop, a barber's . . . an ice house, which receives perhaps more customers
> than any other.

It was inevitable that Bent's Fort would attract competitors. South-central Colorado was an appealing place. The air was salubrious, the

Conestoga wagon, Bent's Fort.

countryside rife with game; close by loomed the Sangre de Cristos and the double profile of the Spanish Peaks. The location, midway between the Mexican settlements to the south, the great buffalo herds to the east, and a string of trading posts to the north along the Platte River, attracted many former mountain men who, after trapping out the beaver on just about every stream west of the hundredth meridian, were looking for a new livelihood. In the early 1840s, at the confluence of Fountain Creek and the Arkansas River (where the city of Pueblo now stands), a group of ex-trappers—among them Mathew Kinkead, George Simpson, John Brown, Jim Beckwourth, and Alexander Barclay—helped construct a rudimentary trading post out of adobe bricks. To make the bricks they brought Mexican workers over the mountains from Taos, thus laying the foundation for the bicultural settlements that later would flourish in the region.

Fontaine-qui-bouille, "Fountain Creek," tumbles out of the Rockies at the foot of Ute Pass behind present-day Colorado Springs before turning south and winding through the foothills and flatlands some 40 miles to a confluence with the Arkansas River. The location was congenial, offering access to three critical resources: grass, wood, and water. The climate was mild and the winters temperate. Unlike Bent's Fort, which boasted high walls and turrets designed for defense, the crude pueblo was less a fort than a typical New Mexican *placita*, built to shelter farm animals and hard-working families. It featured 8-foot walls, squat bastions, and a handful of cramped, stuffy rooms. Early travelers such as Englishman George Ruxton and Bostonian Francis Parkman weren't impressed. "A wretched species of fort," Parkman groused after visiting the place in 1846 and eating a meal off the floor, "miserably cracked and delapidated" (quoted in LeCompte, p. 176). Dr. Benjamin Kern, a member of the 1848 Fremont Expedition, described it even less flatteringly as a "compound of Spaniards, horses mules dogs chickens and bad stench" (quoted in LeCompte, p. 218).

There's a racial undertone to these complaints, generated no doubt by the diversity of ethnic types that flourished at isolated posts such as Pueblo and Bent's Fort. During the heady days of the beaver trade, trappers came from a variety of backgrounds—Anglo-American, French Canadian, Mexican, European. They lived a carefree life, consorting with any native woman who would have them. Once they settled down to farm and trade in places like Pueblo, they usually "married" into an Indian family, especially one from a nearby tribe—Cheyenne, Arapaho, Ute—which linked them with a complex network of potential customers and benefactors. Once they had accumulated a little equity, a few even solidified their newfound respectability by marrying white women from back East and moving into fancy houses with picket fences and lace curtains.

The familial web along the Upper Arkansas in the 1840s and 1850s was complex and diverse. Great Plains historian Elliott West has described it as a kind of "ethnic slumgullion stew, the plains equivalent of a lower east side neighborhood" (West, p. 118). Nearly all the former trappers had Indian wives, some more than one. The mixed-blood children from these alliances would leave their marks, good and bad, on the history of the West. These loose aggregations would in turn be followed by the more orthodox Anglo and Hispanic families, which formed the core of the pioneers who after the Civil War actually transformed the land from wilderness to grassy pasture. In telling contrast to the stereotype of the solitary figure (trapper, cowboy, gunfighter) imposing law and order on a chaotic landscape, families and not individuals were the primary pacifying force in the taming of southeast Colorado.

Not enough has been said about the role of women in the development of frontier posts such as Pueblo. Although Bent's Fort boasted the perfunctory Indian wife and the occasional female visitor from back East such as Susan Magoffin, it remained a bulwark of male dominance; by contrast, women shared the fate and fortunes of the early days of Pueblo almost equally with the men. Teresita Sandoval—beautiful, headstrong, and tempestuous—went through a succession of husbands, emerging stronger, smarter, and tougher from each alliance. She is the prototype of the canny, indomitable female—Indian, Hispanic, and Anglo—who has had, and continues to have, such a positive impact on the Spanish Peaks region. The usurpation of Mexican law by the victorious Anglos at the end of the Mexican War in 1848 worked to the disadvantage of most Hispanic women.

Peacock, parapet, Bent's Fort.

"Under Mexican laws," says historian Deborah Mora-Espinosa, "women could inherit and purchase land and livestock, or share ownership with their husbands. . . . They could pursue their own business interests, and a woman could initiate divorce"—rights most Anglo-American women would not enjoy until the next century (Mora-Espinosa, p. 18).

By 1850 much had changed. The year before, fed up with military meddling, dismayed by the diminution of the great buffalo herds, saddened by the smallpox epidemic that decimated his beloved Cheyenne Indians, William Bent closed the gates to his fort and set fire to the magazine. Seventy miles west, the tawdry pueblo at the confluence of Fountain Creek and the Arkansas River was practically deserted as people dispersed, some to California to search for gold, some to New Mexico, some to the new Mormon enclave on the Great Salt Lake, a few disgruntled ones back to the settlements along the Missouri and Mississippi Rivers. A traveler in 1853 described the place as "a collection of deserted adobe huts at the mouth of the Boiling Spring river" (quoted in LeCompte, p. 225).

No trip to Bent's Fort is complete without a stroll through the bosque shading the banks of the Arkansas River. It's pleasant to walk here, through tall grass edging the steep cut banks, past stands of willow and box elder, listening to cottonwood leaves fluttering overhead. A flat stem enables these leaves to turn 180 degrees in a slight breeze. In the days before air conditioning, people would sit under the trees and bask in the extra breath these shivering leaves stirred up. The wind makes a distinctive sound as it soughs through these gnarly old trees with their thick trunks, splintered branches, and deeply runneled bark. It's easy to imagine hundreds of tipis pitched alongside the path of the river. William Bent reports that in spring of 1842 thousands of Indians from half a dozen tribes were camped up and down the Arkansas within eyeshot of the fort. Bent's Fort was neutral ground, and all animosities, tribal and personal, were suspended for the length of time anyone camped there. In addition to being a skillful merchant, Bent was a first-rate conciliator, and he dealt sternly with those who violated this prohibition. He was married to a Cheyenne woman, and the bonds of his extended family reached far and wide throughout the Indian community. A gathering at Bent's Fort was a time for celebration. There were horse races, powwows, religious ceremonies, and serious trading with the factors at the fort. Young men used this lull in their normal lives to court young women, and at night the reedy tremolo of love flutes could be heard over the barking of dogs and the whinnying of weary horses.

My feet tramp a path toward the faint crinkle of the Arkansas River as it cuts its way east across the thin grassy soil of southeast Colorado. Standing at the edge of the bank, I watch the wrinkly brown surface, stirred by mysterious currents, crack into a thousand pieces and coalesce into a smooth purling flow. Quite possibly the river at this brief juncture a few score yards from the fort's front gate looks much today as it did 160 years ago. The Indians are gone, and all we have left is the sound of the wind creaking through the crowns of these ancient trees and the facsimile of a fort that symbolizes much of what the upstart nation to the east had to offer to the wilderness and the world. But for all its lavish detail, the fort isn't the whole story of this place. These trees contain secrets of another world we can never fully fathom. Deeper, darker, more mysterious than anything we have ever known, or ever will.

Before driving off in my car, I go back to the fort and climb the wooden ladder to the circular parapet at the northwest corner. The peaks are still there, faintly visible, flashing like silver in the fading sun. Bent's Fort is probably the farthest point at which I can locate the Spanish Peaks by line of sight. The fort's history touches on the history of the peaks, and there is a connection, albeit tenuous, I am anxious to explore. Simple observation implies a form of possession; that which I visually connect provides the basis for a future emotional linkup. Later, on Colorado State Highway 10, angling southwest toward Walsenburg, I watch the peaks swell in size with each passing mile. It's good to have discerned them from afar, and now it's equally good to find myself rushing toward them at better than 65 mph.

The physical journeying from one point to the next encapsulates the rhythm of the imaginative trip I experienced at the fort, and the closer I approach the more expectant I become. Those twin snowy crowns betoken the promise of a real wilderness that can accommodate our deepest urges and desires. Bent's Fort represents order and civilization, which in the end were ruthlessly imposed upon the landscape of the West. The bosque embodies the evanescent memory of a people whose lives were once acted out in harmony with the land they lived on. From the parapet of the fort, I am pulled across the grass to the specter of the peaks, which even in their shimmery outline represent freedom and the potential for a more meaningful life. Something else, too, vague and ill defined, a simultaneity of perspective, up close and far away, the encompassing view of a hawk concomitant with the limited perspective of a porcupine. Twin peaks, double perspectives, yin and yang, positive and negative, plus all the other dichotomies that govern the bipolar nature of our bodily identity. I launch myself from the platform of Bent's Fort toward a deeper understanding of these stately mountains, back and forth, back and forth, in a never-ending helix that enables me to experience the same tremor of excitement when viewed 80 miles distant as I feel walking in a grassy meadow near the tree line.

Monument Lake

At the time of the volcanoes, all the water disappeared from the mountains. One by one the people perished of thirst. A chief from a northern tribe journeyed south to find water, while a chief of a southern tribe headed north. They met on the slopes of the Spanish Peaks, and after talking they embraced in friendship. Then, realizing that neither had found water, they commenced to cry—wet, soppy tears that collected in a lake at their feet. Suddenly, a nearby volcano spewed smoke and lava into the air. The two chiefs, still clutched in an embrace, turned to stone. The lake remained, surrounding the chiefs with enough water to silence the volcano and satisfy the thirst of their people.

10
Apishapa Stage House

A dirt road angles east from the town of Aguilar, over the flats toward a curious formation I call Iguana Butte after the dike that protrudes from the center of its back. This dike resembles the toothy dorsal stripe on a Galapagos land iguana. The iguana looks as if it's lying on its stomach facing east, drowsing in the summer heat. The road east of Aguilar rambles in a steady line toward the iguana's posterior. The dike, which originates in the Spanish Peaks, runs underground for several miles before emerging at the foot of the butte and running up over the top. What's an iguana that big doing out here? I ask myself. Now wait a minute, a voice growls in my head, that ain't no iguana out there. That's just a big pile of dirt and rock. Wide open spaces play tricks inside your head. All that emptiness yawning like a slack mouth, enticing the imagination to rush in and fill the void.

It was a hot, dry August afternoon. Dust hung in the air like a speckled curtain. The sun was an oily smudge somewhere off to the west, smeared by a greasy scree of clouds fomented by forest fires way out in the Four Corners. Barbara Sparks and I passed the ruins of several adobe houses; at the gate to the private ranch, which we had permission to enter, two creamy brown-and-white Hereford milk cows with placid faces and pink udders waited patiently for us to let them in.

Inside the gate we bumped over a rutted path. The grass was cropped and mashed. Starchy cow plop splotched the ground amid growths of spiky cholla. We dipped down a steep cut bank and crossed the Apishapa River, the tires of the four-wheel drive vehicle splashing through scummy water. *Apishapa,* a Jicarilla Apache word meaning "stinking water." Out here on the flat, fouled with cow shit, it looked every bit of that. High in the peaks,

Catholic cemetery, Aguilar.

down from Cordova Pass, it bubbled in a clear stream. Out of the foothills it sliced across the plains, cutting deep furrows, an especially deep one at Apishapa Canyon, before trickling into the Arkansas River east of Pueblo.

We spotted the ruins of the stage house tucked inside a grove of cottonwoods. The cottonwoods were old and splintered; downed branches lay everywhere, chunks of flaked bark. A sluggish wind twirled the heart-shaped leaves in a sheeny flash. Cow bones, scorched boards and struts, bits of metal added to the mess. The place smelled of rattlesnakes. I could feel them watching us, testing the air with their sleek tongues. Huge ant heaps bubbled up, alive with stinging insects, adding to the conical pile of their homes. I poked around an adobe outbuilding, most likely an old stable, built of long, narrow straw-flecked bricks with a crumbling roof and deep dirt floor layered with generations of manure. Evidently the Apishapa had undermined it at various times, carrying away the soil that supported its base. A lizard scurried along a splintered board. The late-summer air was sullen and thick. Near a corner of the stable yawned a gigantic badger hole.

There wasn't much left of what once had been a long, rambling, two-story stage house. A pair of reddish-brown adobe brick chimneys stuck up from the halves of the once symmetrical house, divided by an entryway that ran from front to back. The remaining wall sections leaned away from each

Iguana-shaped butte and dike
east of Aguilar.

other, revealing gaping cracks. The whole thing looked as if a stiff wind might collapse it like a house of cards. Several walls had been plastered with protective facades into which recent visitors had gouged their names and initials. Peppery nicks splattered the facades—target practice, no doubt. A photo from the early 1900s (reproduced in Dotson, p. 1) shows a sturdy roof, tall chimneys, four windows up and down, a balcony running around the second story—a genteel touch, indicative of the culture of the man who built it. A considerable edifice for this part of the world. A once thriving place reduced to a desiccated husk. A sad hulk of distinctly southern vintage, built of adobe and accoutered with wood—struts, supports, veranda, window jambs, decayed lintels—very little of which remained.

A colorful fellow named Col. James Allen Foster built the house between 1870 and 1872. Foster served in the Confederate cavalry during the Civil War. He is described by a descendent as "a kindly gentleman from Virginia, a jovial and congenial host, a wit and something of a reconoteur [sic]" (Dotson, p. 1). He was definitely a hard drinker and an unreconstructed rebel. During a Fourth of July celebration in the town of Trinidad, as the band paraded down Main Street playing the Yankee tune "Marching Through Georgia," Colonel Foster rumbled out to confront the bandmaster. "Yes, damn you!" he roared. "You marched through Georgia when there were

Ruins of stage house on Apishapa River, built by James Allen Foster.

only women and children and men so old they couldn't shoulder a gun" (Dotson, p. 1).

At the close of that bitter conflict, Foster returned to his home in Virginia to find everything in ruins. A new life beckoned in the West, so he and his wife packed up and headed out. A contingent of Georgia miners led by William Green Russell had panned for gold up and down the Colorado Front Range in the 1850s, with some encouraging success. Word about the possibilities of a new life in southern Colorado spread throughout the South after 1865. The climate was healthy, there was plenty of timber, the grass down in the narrow canyons was suitable for grazing, there might even be gold in the depths of the Spanish Peaks. And so they came, first in dribbles, then in droves, entire families looking for a chance, a notch, a foothold, something by which they might lever themselves onto the track of a more rewarding life. Known loosely as the "Georgia Colony" after the example set by Russell, they settled on homesteads along watercourses such as the Apishapa, within easy reach of the brooding double peaks Ute Indians called Wah-to-yah, "Breasts of the World."

Timbering wasn't Colonel Foster's forte; he was a Virginian after all, and soon after arriving on the banks of the Apishapa he purchased a few head of cattle. As a former cavalryman, the colonel fancied himself a connoisseur of fine horseflesh. He is credited with being the first man in Las Animas County to own a string of well-bred driving horses. He proudly named his horses after famous Confederate generals and prominent Democrats. Within a few years he was one of the biggest cattlemen in the county.

The region was still untamed in the early 1870s. In the fall parties of Ute Indians came down from the mountains to hunt antelope, elk, and the few buffalo that still grazed the slopes. Some of the Utes had adopted the white man's ways; a native sheep rancher on a nearby spread refused to keep his animals from straying onto Foster's land. Foster and his adopted son rode over one day to teach the infidel a lesson, only to be chased off by a well-aimed arrow that buried itself deep in the withers of the colonel's horse. How the colonel exacted his final revenge on the upstart Indian is not recorded.

The town of Trinidad was the closest provisioning place, and settlers like Foster usually laid in supplies to last the winter. Steak cost twenty-five cents for 2 pounds, chewing tobacco three dollars for 12 pounds. It took a team of four horses to haul forty dollars worth of groceries back to the banks of the Apishapa. Foster and his first wife, Susan, had no children, though they later adopted several.

It seemed only fitting that the colonel drift into the hospitality business. He exhibited all the characteristics of a born innkeeper—warmth, congeniality, bibulous charm, a boisterous sense of humor. He was a memorable storyteller, he loved gossip, he knew everyone in that part of the country. "His only enemy," according to his descendent, "was John Barleycorn" (Dotson, p. 3). But who on a wintry night, with the wind howling and the horses tucked snugly away in the stable, could refuse a wee drammie from a slight bearded man whose light-colored eyes lit up with mischief and hilarity at the close of another raucous tale?

An ad that appeared in the Pueblo *Chieftain* on May 1, 1872, set the tone for an establishment already renown for its hospitality and fine food:

> James A. Foster at the Apishapa Station 20 miles north of Trinidad is always prepared to accomodate the travelling public in a manner not surpassed anywhere in southern Colorado. A traveler may rely upon finding comfortable rooms, good beds, and the very best of meals.
>
> There is an excellent stable with an abundance of the best hay and grain always on hand where all stock entrusted to me will be well cared for.
>
> Jas. A. Foster

For a couple of decades the Apishapa Stage House was the center of conviviality for the area, a gathering place not only for paying guests but for all manner of local people—miners, timbermen, trappers, and freighters—who sat on the balcony or inside by one of the four fireplaces exchanging gossip and news.

It was also an important changeover for weary horses and men travel-ing the dusty trails in the shadow of the Spanish Peaks. The Foster Stage Station was one of the main stops along the north-south trail between Pueblo, Colorado, and Santa Fe, New Mexico. The stagecoaches, usually of the Concord type, carried four armed men to ward off Indians and bandits. Their arrival was announced by rifle shots. A few minutes later, amid a rolling cloud of dust and the barking of dogs and the yelling of commands, the stage rattled into the yard, reeking of sweaty horses, passengers, and leather harnessing. If it was late the passengers spent the night, along with the crew and guards; they were treated to a tasty meal served by Susan Foster, the colonel's wife—by all accounts a first-rate frontier chef—and later a few convivial cups by the venerable colonel. Eventually the extension of the Denver & Rio Grande Railroad south from Walsenburg to Trinidad spelled the end of this remarkable hostelry. By the early 1880s the stage lines were gone, and Foster converted the house into a hotel and home for tuberculosis patients.

Susan Foster died April 15, 1889. Her death was a severe blow to the colonel, who sought to assuage his grief by journeying back to Virginia for the first time since 1866 to look for another wife. He went with a suitcase full of money, which he spent freely. We have a photo of him taken about this time, looking white-whiskered and slump-shouldered and smooth-browed, with a devilish glint in his eyes (reproduced in Dotson, p. 2). Two years later he returned again to Virginia, where he met and married a Miss Margaret Elizabeth Alderson, age fifty-three. (The colonel was sixty-five.) The second Mrs. Foster had experience in the hotel business, which she put to good use in her new sanitorium/rest home tucked away in a grove of trees near the banks of the Apishapa River in far-off Colorado. Colonel Foster appears to have lived contentedly at the stage house until he passed away on October 1, 1895. Margaret Foster survived until 1908.

The graveyard was located a quarter-mile due west of the house on a slight rise near the river. We drove past grazing cattle, mostly Herefords, with their backs to the dull dripping sun. Birds were surprisingly plentiful: mead-owlarks, doves, lark buntings, western kingbirds with lemon-yellow tails, loggerhead shrikes with their distinctive black tails, waiting patiently on shrubs for some victim to appear.

The graveyard lay in the shadow of the peaks, located straight west, east peak rising dainty and proud, west peak looming higher and bulkier behind it, both indistinct and blurry in the late afternoon heat. Tiny juniper saplings took hold across the trampled grass. To the east, a sweeping view of the flatlands. Clouds of grasshoppers took flight ahead of our flailing feet as we climbed to the top of the cemetery. The grass, dry and crackly, was like a carpet of starched, combustible paper.

The colonel's alabaster-white tombstone was easy to find:

James A. Foster
Col. 8 VA Cav CSA

Tombstone, Col. James Allen Foster CSA.

Close by, a slim black marble obelisk with two sets of names etched on opposite sides: Susan Foster 1833–1889, and Margaret Elizabeth Foster, Wife of J.A. Foster 1838–1908 (the last one exercising her option to define her role for posterity).

Maybe it was the day, the streaky air, the filmy shapes of the peaks congealing to the west, the hint of ineffable distances to the east; whatever, the place seemed wretched and forlorn. A dry, fluttery wind teased our ears. We saw more ant heaps, lizards, chitinous stinkbugs, and hairy black spiders. Yucca and prickly pear stuck up between loose pebbles and rocks. A hot place, astringent, imbued with a kind of brittle nobility, the resting place of a type of people whose courage we can only guess at. We poked about for a while, looking at every legible tombstone:

> Christian Calderon
> died at Aguilar
> August 18, 1895
> Aged 2 years

> Robert Bayles
> Born
> Sept. 22, 1829
> Died
> Dec. 16, 1899
> FATHER

> We Loved Him
> JOHN
> Nov. 1, 1851
> died
> Sept. 25, 1900
> FARRELL

At the base, an illegible inscription. Someone had placed a sprig of faded plastic violets there, propped against a tiny splintered cross. What constitutes a proper life? Memories, stories, the echo of a snapping stick. The detritus of a vibrant physicality, winnowed to these bare facts.

We got back in the shiny black four-wheel drive and chugged out of there.

The Demons of Gold

Long before the white man arrived, gold was mined in the Huajatolla and was used to decorate the shrines and altars of the deities who ruled the kingdoms of Mexico. As they watched the precious metal trickle south to the fabulous courts of Nezhuatcoyotl, the gods became jealous. They installed demons on the slopes of the double mountain who spat fire and smoke and forbade all men to approach.

No more gold came from Huajatolla, and thereafter all those seeking gold on the twin peaks were cursed.

11
Bullseye Mine

I'm sitting on a steep slope of shattered rock deep inside a bowl-shaped cirque, high above the tree line on West Spanish Peak. It's early afternoon—streaky, overcast. A few dark clouds are starting to gather along the west rim. We've been climbing since seven-thirty—for the past two hours over a scree of cracked and broken stones, our feet pressing loose rock together with the faint click of billiard balls. Click clack click clock. A strange percussive sound, subtly unnerving. There's nothing quite so rigorous as hauling your body up a sharp incline against the implacable weight of gravity. A refrain by Samuel Beckett from one of his novels, "I can't go on . . . I'll go on," plays repeatedly in my head. Climbing is like surgery or a divorce; you want it over as soon as possible.

The air at this altitude (around 12,000 ft.) is cool, silvery, and light. My winded lungs suck it in. I've gone about as far as I intend to go. Several of the others in our little party have forged on to the back wall of the cirque. I'm content to sit and look around, perched on a rock on a steep slope overlooking a snow-packed fissure cut by a spring-fed stream that issues higher up across the way from under a scaly bulge of damp rocks.

It's a precarious world above the tree line. One feels so vulnerable and exposed. Fortunately, a layer of clouds has filtered out the worst of the sun's rays. Everything that grows or moves up here has to find a nourishing crack between the rubble of broken rock. Take that alpine fern, for example, snugged down in a moist sliver of dark, grainy dirt. A little while ago I saw a vole scamper across a boulder. Slim pickings for even that enterprising creature, but somehow it muddles through, helped by a long hibernative respite under several feet of snow when its heart rate drops to

Glacier-gouged cirques, West
Spanish Peak. Bullseye Mine
tucked away in cirque on left.

an occasional ping and it dreams uncharted dreams no one else can possibly know.

The weight of a glacier formed this bowl-like depression, or cirque. I try to imagine what that must have looked like, say, 15,000 years ago. I can't. There are certain phenomena that can't be visualized with a mortal eye. I do know that once the ice started to melt, it must have created a colossal mess down below. The ice was laced with nutrients and minerals, good for the grass in the foothills. The amount of meltwater that thundered down these slopes must have been astounding. Accompanied by huge chunks of ice that ripped and roared, carrying off groves of dark trees in a crackling, popping crescendo. And then pooling in the lower valleys, saturating the vales and depressions, feeding the grasses, herbs, and forbs, which, when the water ran off, rose under the warm prompting of the sun. To be trod underfoot by the megafauna that once roamed these parts—sloths, tapirs, woolly mammoths, bison antiquus—whose presence attracted the hunters with their atlatls and lanceolate spear points; who lured them deep into the soggy places and hacked and pierced them till they died.

I tried to imagine this steep-sided basin packed with giant chunks of ice, the massive drainage that occurred as the temperature warmed and water slipped out in countless rivulets, widening to a thunderous gush as the ice calved off in jagged clumps and roared down below, carrying everything with it. On the way up to this desolate eyrie, toiling like a Beckett character across a propless stage, I spotted several sumps where huge sections of rock had broken off and disappeared downhill. The rock cloaking the sides of the entire summit of the west peak is like the shattered skin of a granite skull. Everything here, despite its stolid appearance, is in a perpetual state of decomposition. This rock, which we count on for stability and repose, is in the process of being worn down to a proverbial nub. Well, it's all about gravity, whether here or down on the flats. Gravity as the centering force of our lives, anchoring us to places we don't always want to be. Gravity, the reductio ad absurdum of every hope or aspiration. First ice, then rock, snow, rain, it doesn't matter. Everything eventually ends up down below. West Spanish Peak appears in danger of losing its crown with little hope of replenishment. Loss of its cracked integument results in a progressive thickening at the waist. Gravity, then, as a kind of chronic middle-age crisis.

We're here to look for evidence of the old Bullseye Mine. So far, we've found only one minor shaft. A few splintered timbers, a rock-choked opening out from which spirals a faint gasp of cool air, cooler than the alpine air outside, which I find curious. My imagination conjures mephitic vapors forged in the depths, tainted with sulphur, the stink of a subterranean bellows.

For all the stories that swirl around the peaks regarding fabulous troves of silver and gold, few people have ever struck it rich. The Spanish poked around, but whether they ever scored big has been lost in the misty ether of legend and myth. In the late nineteenth century a new mineral, coal, caught the fancy of speculators. Unlike the solitary prospector with his pick and pan, coal mining was a high-profile industry requiring lots of workers and major capitalization. The region literally glimmered with black, glistening beds, especially around the drier piñon and juniper slopes at the foot of the peaks, which companies began to probe in the 1870s. Miners of many nationalities filtered into the region, further complicating the racial and ethnic makeup of the population. No doubt they heard the stories, and as they picked at the dark seams below the surface, who among these sturdy immigrants seeking to make their fortune in the New World could resist dreaming about some dazzling mother lode concealed under the rocky summits of the grandiose peaks soaring over their heads?

High up on the north slope of West Spanish Peak, the citizens of the new town of La Veta launched a community venture known as the Bullseye Mine. They built a road through dense forest and hauled up the latest machinery. Many locals sank their entire savings into the enterprise. Enough ore was finally extracted to transport to the mills in Pueblo, 60 miles north. A reliable lad named Billie Hamilton was chosen to drive the wagon. Billie lived at Francisco Fort with his young wife. That memorable day he came down from the mountain in a creaky wagon spilling over with ore, he stopped at the fort long enough to bid his wife farewell. "Wife," he reportedly said, "you can hang up that dish towel now. You won't have to wash no dishes anymore. We're all rich. We've struck it rich" (quoted in McLelland, p. 16).

With that he waved goodbye and headed north on the long journey to Pueblo. His thoughts were consumed with how his life would change once he cashed in the hot chips stacked high in the wagon. In Pueblo a few days later, he dropped off some samples at the assayer's office just to verify how much gold they really contained. Then he went shopping. When he returned to the office, he was dumbfounded to hear the news. "I'm mighty sorry to tell you," the assayer said, "but there isn't a trace of gold in that rock you just brought me."

What does it mean to dig into the side of a mountain in search of riches? What portion of our hidden selves lies locked in this mass of stone? Today we're not as interested in converting raw ore into cash, and so we look for something else. But were this 1900 instead of 2000, the people in our little party would be thinking about gold. Consider the Spanish. They trekked all over the Southwest looking for it. Such a landscape—hammered like an anvil by the blazing sun, edged along its chimerical distances by flat-topped mesas and snow-capped peaks—spawned a host of glib fabulists. Tough, pragmatic men who should have known better succumbed to the lure and added their own versions to stories as evanescent as the arid winds that chapped their pale, droopy faces. A bag of windy fabrications was duly transformed into an agenda of imperial policy. Wherever a Spaniard went in this amazing new world, the mania for gold went with him.

Once bitten by the bug, there is no cure. I'm old enough to remember the uranium craze of the 1950s, and although I grew up in the Midwest, I remember stories about local families taking vacations in Arizona and New Mexico to look for uranium. You could buy uranium detection kits in the hardware stores. Everybody was daft about uranium. Few people knew about its lethal properties, and those who did weren't telling. People just knew that it was needed to power the nuclear plants, bombs, submarines, and aircraft carriers that sprang up across America during the Eisenhower years.

But my reverie was disturbed by the sight of more clouds forming over the cirque's west rim. Barbara Sparks shot me a worried look. "We need to get off this mountain," she said.

Shortly after we started down, a ferocious hailstorm began. The air was suddenly clotted with pelting sheets of marble-sized hailstones that stung as they struck bare skin. The first clap of thunder gripped me with a dread I haven't experienced in a long time. Lightning crackled, followed by a second detonation, this one like an air burst almost directly overhead. Nowhere to hide, nothing to crouch behind. I reviewed the emergency procedures, which consisted of one simple motion: as soon as the hair on the back of your neck curls up, hit the deck and spread your body like an amoeba across the rocks. It won't do much good, as lightning finds its way into the teeniest crack, but I kept thinking of this as I tripped down the path of wet, broken stones praying that I wouldn't slip and break my ankle. CRASH! POW! There's no video of that descent, for which I'm grateful, but I know I did the whole thing on my toes, tremulous with fear, flapping my short arms like a chicken in the face of a hungry fox. In a matter of minutes the entire slope was coated with tiny white ice balls. We ducked and danced and slithered and slipped but managed to make it to the tree line just as the hail slacked off and the skies began to clear. I paused to calm my heaving lungs and gulp a little water. "All mountains walk with their toes on all waters and splash there," says Zen Master Dōgen. Well, I just walked, splashing, with mine, not with much grace, more in the manner of a herniated goat, but down I got, grateful, happy, ready to call it a day.

The Twelve Chests of Gold

Around 1700, a Spanish regiment marched out of Santa Fe bound for the Spanish garrison at St. Augustine, Florida. The regiment escorted twelve chests of gold with which to pay the soldiers stationed at that far-off post. The regiment was commanded by Carrasco Rodriguez, who ignored his guides and marched northeast instead of southeast. Winter found them near the present site of Trinidad, Colorado, where they holed up until spring. When spring came they marched on in the wrong direction.

The regiment was never heard from again. Five years later a dying Apache revealed that the entire command had been killed in an ambush. Bits of armor and other equipment were found in various Apache encampments. Years later an entire suit of armor was discovered near the Purgatoire River.

Some think the Spanish buried the chests along the banks of the river. Others think they may have dumped them into the water. Whatever, there's a good chance that twelve chests of Spanish gold remain concealed somewhere along the Purgatoire River.

12
La Veta 3

In the three-sided square that forms the *placita* at Francisco Fort in the heart of the little town of La Veta there's a tall cottonwood with wide-spreading branches that towers over all the other trees in the yard. The tree reputedly was planted by Col. John Francisco in 1878, presumably to give shade to the wagons, people, and stock corralled inside the *placita*; but it gained its real notoriety as a place from which bandits and desperados were summarily hanged during the early pioneer days, seventeen in all, so the story goes.

Although it's questionable whether any villains died at the end of a rope dangling from one of the branches, the tree today exhibits great dignity and antiquity; ah, if those branches could talk, what stories they might tell! Usually, as cottonwoods age they become brittle and fragmented, but the Francisco Fort tree appears healthy and robust. The circumference near the base measures nearly 19 feet; the bark, deeply runneled and grooved, appears tightly attached to the trunk and limbs. The tree exudes an aura of nobility and veneration; in some ways it is the last living survivor of the early pioneer days along the Upper Cuchara River Valley.

By 1870 tiny settlements, sometimes no more than a cluster of tents or brush *jacales,* had sprung up along the four major rivers that drain the Spanish Peaks region. On the Huerfano, two and a half miles upriver from the solitary butte that protrudes like a dark pimple off the surface of the plains, were Badito and St. Mary's. On the Cuchara, in addition to Francisco Fort, were Oso, Hermanes Plaza, Tequisite, and La Plaza de los Leones. On the Apishapa were Gonzales (later known as Aguilar), Augusta, and Colonel Foster's Stage House. And on the Purgatoire there was the embryonic

The "hanging tree" at Francisco Fort.

village of Trinidad, settled by Felipe Baca, a hard-working teamster who got his start hauling supplies for gold miners on the Colorado Front Range.

In 1858 Don Miguel Antonio Leon, along with a family named Atencio, settled on the north side of the Cuchara River in a little community they called la Plaza de los Leones. They threw up modest dwellings on both sides of an old Indian trail that today, known as Main Street, runs through the center of Walsenburg. In 1861—the year Colorado was declared a territory—Huerfano County was formed. As the decade progressed, the severity

Territorial trim, Baca House, Trinidad, built in 1870.

of the winters in the nearby San Luis Valley, coupled with Ute Indian raids, sent many settlers packing over the Sangre de Cristos to the milder climate and safer haven of the Cuchara Valley. Between 1865 and 1869, these new settlers were joined by an influx of Hispanic immigrants from Abiquiu, Taos, Española, and other New Mexico towns.

In 1870 a German immigrant named Fred Walsen came to Plaza de los Leones. He established a trading post and soon became a community leader. So strong was his influence, so successful his ideas for development that in 1873, after the town was officially platted, it was named Walsenburg in his honor. The following year the Huerfano County seat was transferred there.

In 1876 the Denver & Rio Grande Railroad reached Walsenburg and pushed a spur west to the site of Francisco Fort (soon to be renamed La Veta). With the Indian threat almost totally removed, the east wall and part of the south wall of the fort were torn down to allow the new railroad into the plaza. The depot was established here; a small turntable was installed to wheel the tiny narrow gauge engines around and point them back out. A hotel operated on the premises, along with several other commercial ventures. The next year the depot was moved several blocks north, taking the business section with it; and although the fort retained its commercial viability for many years afterward, it never regained its importance as the community hub.

In 1876 Fred Walsen, sensing the economic potential of coal mining in the region, leased the land west of Walsenburg and enticed the Colorado Coal and Iron Company, forerunner of Colorado Fuel & Iron, to open the Walsen Mine. M. Beshoar, author of a history of Las Animas County, deemed the coal around both Trinidad and Walsenburg as "superior in quality, free from sulphur, hard and compact in structure, rich in carbon, well-suited to all manufacturing and domestic purposes." Other mines soon followed, and like blackbirds to a field of freshly cut corn, people from all over the country began to flock to the Spanish Peaks.

Hiram Vasquez, the man who helped John Francisco and Henry Daigre build Francisco Fort, settled in La Veta. Vasquez's life stands as a testament to the lives of practically every pioneer in the region. The land may have been promising, but the life was harsh, riddled with heartbreak and despair. (Vasquez's first wife died, along with ten of his thirteen children.) Vasquez reflected the changes, some subtle, some profound, all significant, that accompanied the metamorphosis of the region from wilderness to settlement. In October 1874 in the new town of Walsenburg, Vasquez became a member of the local Masonic Lodge. Twice a month, dressed in a dark suit with a crisp white shirt buttoned at the collar, he rode a mule from La Veta to Walsenburg to attend meetings—the same man who, eleven years earlier, had slipped over the wall of beleaguered Francisco Fort and made his way, also by mule, 120 miles east to the military post of Fort Lyon.

Fortunately, through Zella Rae Albright's absorbing biography, *One Man's Family: The Life of Hiram Vasquez, 1843–1939,* we can follow the

Huerfano County Courthouse, Walsenburg.

Caboose, Denver & Rio Grande
Railroad.

course of this remarkable man as he evolved from Indian fighter to early
settler to entrepreneur to ancestral survivor, dying finally in 1939 at age
ninety-six. As an old man he used to sit on the porch of his house in La
Veta, gazing with transparent blue eyes at the twin peaks rising to the south.
"I remember when them mountains were nothing but holes in the ground,"
he'd say with a sly chuckle to anyone who'd listen (Albright, p. 299).

Along the way he endured terrible torments. On April 25, 1884, Hiram
Vasquez Jr., age two years, ten months, died of pneumonia. The grieving
parents carried the tiny casket to the La Veta cemetery and laid it to rest
with their own hands. Martha, Vasquez's second wife, pregnant with her
third child, nearly went out of her mind. Hiram decided to move—not
away from the Spanish Peaks, never that, but over to the south side to
the budding Hispanic town of Gonzales (soon to be known as Aguilar)
on the banks of the Apishapa River, where he settled in for a while as a
storekeeper.

To someone like Hiram, who'd been adopted into the Shoshone tribe
and who had known the real wildness of the West, life in this new, settled,
mechanized climate with its expanding grid of roads, telegraph poles, and
railroad tracks must have been bewildering indeed. On May 31, 1883, the
Huerfano (County) Herald reported that the Denver & Rio Grande Rail-

road had achieved a record run from Pueblo south to Cuchara Junction (just east of Walsenburg), a distance of 46 miles in 49 minutes—a trip that used to take two days, sometimes longer, in a heavy wagon. Another item that year in the same newspaper sounded a disturbing note. Responding to pressures from local merchants, the city council of Pueblo ordered the biggest known cottonwood in the state of Colorado—88 feet tall, 26 feet in circumference at the base, with tree rings indicating an age of 380 years—to be cut down because it interfered with horse-drawn wagons and buggies in the middle of the 200 block of South Union Avenue.

They were made of different stuff back then. Henry L. Sefton, an early settler, ushering a caravan of pack mules along the Cuchara River, had a finger crushed by a sharp hoof. Undeterred, he strolled into a blacksmith shop and placed a spike with a flat point against the bleeding digit. When the first blow from the blacksmith's hammer failed to sever the finger, Sefton coolly turned his hand over and uttered a little sigh as the blacksmith brought the hammer down a second time. The severed finger quivered like a worm and dribbled off the anvil to the floor.

In 1876, engineers for the Denver & Rio Grande Railroad pioneered a path over old La Veta Pass, west of Spanish Peaks, the highest elevation (9,339 ft.) reached by any railroad at that time. The ascent of 2,369 feet covered a distance of 14 miles, an average gain of 160 feet per mile, over "muleshoe curves," said one reporter, "which clung to the shoulders of the dizzy mountains like the strand of a spider's web" (quoted in McLelland, p. 21). The new route linked the Spanish Peaks and the San Luis Valley not only to important markets in Colorado Springs and Denver but also to cities in the Midwest and on the Atlantic seaboard.

By 1880 La Veta (pop. 400) was booming. The town boasted nine saloons and two churches. Tent camps clustered at the edge of town over-flowed with railroad workers. Conditions in the camps were deplorable. Smallpox raged, carrying off scores of workers; officials responded by plac-ing the entire La Veta area under quarantine. Nobody could come in or go out. Work on the railroad sputtered to a halt, business in the saloons lan-guished, people traipsed the muddy streets holding scented kerchiefs to their faces, but gradually the disease burned itself out and life returned to normal.

The Spanish Peaks region was like a gigantic cornucopia, spilling forth promises of every sort. Cattle barons drove their herds across the flatlands east of the peaks and down into the canyons of the Huerfano, Apishapa, and Purgatoire Rivers, where they fattened on the rich mix of grasses. Geologists registered the sites of numerous coal deposits on both sides of the peaks, which miners would soon displace with dynamite and pickax. Both mining and railroad construction created a huge demand for timber, which everyone with an ax and saw and a team of horses pitched in to satisfy. Speculators probed for gold and silver on the slopes of the strange double mountain, whose appeal went much deeper than the mineral riches lodged within its depths.

It doesn't matter if anyone actually dangled in death from the limbs of the venerable cottonwood standing in Francisco Fort. The image is part of our heritage, part of the price we had to pay to convert this feral land to the edenic garden of our cloistered immigrant dreams. In the early days justice lagged behind violence in many western settlements, and before proper authority was established, locals frequently took it upon themselves to rectify criminal activity by the equally criminal expedient of vigilante action. Unlike the Canadian West where red-coated mounted police, representing the British Crown and an established system of jurisprudence, invariably preceded any effort at settlement, parts of the American West for a brief but memorable period endured virtual anarchy because of the absence of uniform laws and the power to enforce them.

Two examples in the Spanish Peaks region will suffice. In 1876 a disgruntled Hispanic laborer brutally murdered pioneer John Brown and his family, a horrific crime that culminated in the man being hanged by a mob outside La Veta. In January 1883 a man named James Lee entered the sawmill of a man named James Wilder on the banks of the Apishapa River and commenced blazing away with a six-shooter. Wilder was badly wounded in the spree. Lee was pursued by a howling mob and apprehended. He was put under guard to await the arrival of police officers from Trinidad, but the mob broke into the log hut where he was confined and riddled him with bullets. In the graphic manner of newspapers of the day, a reporter wrote, "Brains and pieces of head were blown all over the side of the log shanty" (quoted in Albright, p. 206).

The length of time this chaos persisted differed with each new town; despite its story value, the "hanging tree" in La Veta remains more symbolic than rooted in actual fact. Nonetheless, that brief era plagues us to this day. Over the decades, as time has distanced us from historical fact, we have come to romanticize that effort and blow it grotesquely out of proportion. The hanging tree, like the lone gunman, is a pernicious stereotype that denies the reality of so many other crucial factors in the settling of the West—women, minorities, Indians, children, weather, geology, animals, and plant life. The world is so much more complex than we can ever truthfully admit. We yearn to simplify, to bind up these complexities in a single appealing image that will somehow, truthful or not, make sense of a history whose meaning continues to dance just beyond our fingertips.

John Hatcher Encounters the Devil Deep Inside the Spanish Peaks

John Hatcher, fur trapper and mountain man, was riding his mule around the foot of the Spanish Peaks when the mule suddenly balked. Two creatures with long tails, wearing red coats spangled with brass buttons, suddenly appeared and led Hatcher and the mule into a tunnel deep inside the peaks. A blaze of light lit up the tunnel; fiddles screeched; people hooted and hollered.

A hunchbacked boy with bulbous gray eyes led the mule away. Hatcher was greeted by an elderly man wearing a black coat and gold-wire spectacles. The man offered him a cigar, which he ignited with the tip of his finger. "Yore the devil hisself!" Hatcher roared. "The very same," the man replied and ushered Hatcher into a room reeking of sulfur and brimstone where an old trapper Hatcher once knew was being tortured by a gang of fiends who scorched his blistered flesh with hot irons. The Devil then led him down a long flight of steps to a room full of slavering dogs, jibbering imps, and snakes with red tongues and bloodshot eyes. Hatcher nearly fainted with fear, but the Devil offered him a sip from a black flask, which pumped up his courage. Hatcher promptly straddled one of the snakes, called to the fiends to climb on behind him, and commenced to ride the snake like a bronco. The next thing he knew he was inside a burning room packed with screaming devils playing cards who promptly fleeced him of all his money. A preacher whom Hatcher once knew was lodged in a cell in a corner, his wrists bound by chains, the flesh worn down to the bone. "If I'd only acted as I told others to do I wouldn't be here now," he moaned.

Hatcher found an open place in the rock wall, slipped through, and started to run, pursued by dogs, fiends, imps, snakes, and owls. They caught up with him and he rolled down into a canyon, the creatures biting and pummeling, Hatcher biting and punching back, when all of a sudden he was rescued by a party of mountain men who scattered the fiends and slapped their wet hats in his face to bring him around. Hatcher woke out of a drunken stupor to find himself lying along the banks of the Purgatoire River, the bottle of whiskey he had emptied before passing out smashed to flinders against a tree. "The devils from hell was after me," he gasped to his rescuers. "This hos has seen moren he ever wants to agin."

13
Will Prator

A laconic fellow, tall, rangy, pensive, and composed. He speaks in evenly measured beats—slow, steady, unhurried. You can hear the country in his voice, an older, gentler accent.

"I was born in 1955 in Denver. My mother went up there to see her sister, and that's where I come out. But I always thought of La Veta as my home. Here's where I grew up. Soon as she had me, she come back down here."

We're sitting at the kitchen table in his house on the west side of town. Will has just dished up two bowls of elk meat chili and heated tortillas to soak up the juice. It's Friday evening, end of the week, and we're both hungry. Outside, the wind has picked up, and now it's blasting through the yard, shaking the trees as if they were pom-poms. "What's that all about?" he asks, looking out the back door at the dust rising off the grassless yard.

While he talks, I scribble notes. Tomorrow is the first day of black-powder elk hunting season, and Will is excited. Like many La Vetans, he has hunted all his life. Deer and elk taken in the fall traditionally provide a steady source of protein during the long winter months.

"My grandfather, Roy Clifford Spangler, killed the last prairie wolf in the Spanish Peaks. That was back in 1923. The wolf's name was Three Toes. She was known all over Las Animas County. She'd killed more than her share of cows and calves, and the ranchers wanted her gone. Roy was a professional bounty hunter. Other hunters had tried to track her down. Aside from snipping off a few toes, no one had got close. Roy caught her in a trap out on the flats east of Trinidad. He was by himself, and he had to muzzle her on his own with baling wire. It's a good thing he did 'cause she

Will Prator with bear-claw necklace.

gave one last lunge and hit him in the Adam's apple and knocked him clear off his feet. If she hadn't been muzzled, she'd've ripped his throat from ear to ear. Roy said they both had to rest after that. 'We just lay there lookin' at one another,' he said. 'Me on the ground and her on the ground, both of us panting.'"

Every family has its defining story, and this is Will's. The event was recorded in the local newspapers, and people talked about it for years. "It's writ up in several books about the region. On the strength of that achievement, he got steady work with U.S. Fish and Wildlife." Will stands up from the table and disappears into his bedroom. A moment later he returns with a handful of grainy black-and-white photos of Three Toes and his grandfather.

"The wolf lived a few days before she died. Roy tended her, but she was too far gone and finally gave up. That's her with her foot in the trap. And that's her later at the house. People came for miles to have a look."

I examine a photo of Roy Spangler taken about this time. A slight man with an open, honest face—wide mouth, full lips, strong, appealing features. A shock of hair dangles over his pale forehead. He wears coveralls, a denim shirt, and dark tie. He gazes forthrightly into the camera without the slightest hint of self-consciousness. His family was originally from Missouri.

Roy had four daughters; Will's mother was the oldest. She was born and raised in a sod dugout east of Trinidad. When she was eight her mother died of the "black pox," a virulent form of smallpox. The bunkhouse where they lived was quarantined; no one could go in or out. Once a day the children were brought to the house where they could look at their mother through a cloudy glass pane. About the time (1923) Roy killed Three Toes, Will's mother and her sisters were sent back to Missouri to live with the two sets of grandparents.

"Roy died when I was about six. He lived with my mother and stepfather during his declining years, and I used to listen to his stories. I guess that's why I wanted to hunt and trap myself. That and the fact that my stepfather, Ernie Proctor, was a fine hunter too. Ernie grew up on a ranch south of La Veta. He was third or fourth generation, from Georgia colony folks who came to the Spanish Peaks following the War Between the States. He took me out when I was about five or six. For ten years after I graduated from high school in 1973 I hunted and trapped with Ernie. We caught coyote, beaver, bobcat, gray fox, ermine, muskrat, badger. Our best year, 1978–1979, we made $11,000."

Fur prices began to slide in the early 1980s. The big ranches on which they'd done so much trapping and hunting were sold off and subdivided. Accompanying this was a change in attitude; the traditional hunting ethic Will had grown up with came under assault. A new mentality crept down the Front Range to the Spanish Peaks from Denver, Colorado Springs, and Boulder. He began to hear negative things about what he did for a living.

"I was never ashamed of what I did. I done it all my life, my whole family had. It was our livelihood, and we never took anything for granted. We respected these animals; they gave up their lives so we could live. That's the way it's been around here since time began. And now suddenly people were getting on our case. Well, for a while I was a real hardass. When somebody took me to task, I gave it right back. At that time in my life it was hard to understand. I was dealing directly with Mother Nature. I was the first-line person in the trenches. I did the mining, the logging, and hunting. Most people just can't accept the fact that stuff comes from stuff. To strike a spark you got to use both flint and steel. Flint on flint won't get the fire lit. Well, I'm the guy who goes out and lights the fire. The rest of the world goes to the store."

There's no bitterness in his voice, no rancor or anger. He speaks evenly, almost in a monotone, tilting his head now and then to underscore what he has to say. "I couldn't trap today," he concludes. "The whole climate has changed. There's just too many people against it."

Will was raised a Protestant. During the decade he spent trapping and hunting he went through an intense native phase. He dressed like a mountain man, he wore buckskin and moccasins and a long beard, his hair hung down to the middle of his back. He toted a full medicine bag that had been blessed by a Lakota Indian pipe carrier. "I needed that kind of support back then," he tells me after dinner over coffee, "and it worked for me. Not so much now. This past year I been going through a lot of changes. I bought a new Bible, and I been attending church. Because I chose to be a trapper in this life, it stands to reason that I musta been one in a former life."

He looks at me across the table with a fixed, steady gaze. He won't be hurried or rushed; this is the story of his life, and he's letting it out at his own sweet pace and whim. Outside, the wind has died down. The dark of a late-summer evening has settled over the yard and trees like a soft, comforting blanket.

"Each animal we ever took had its own individuality. Down in Apishapa Canyon one time we caught a big bobcat that pulled the log drag away from the set maybe 30 or 40 feet. The cat had got hung up in some cholla and was lying on its back." Will leaned back in his chair and imitated the animal, wiggling his hands in front of his chest and rolling his eyes. "I thought he was dead, so I reached out over his face to release the jaws of the trap when I saw him blink. Well, I want to tell you something. The world came together at that instant at the end of a pin. It was all there, my entire life included. I reeled back, but the cat didn't strike. I don't know whether he was warning me or whether he was just too weak to strike. All I know is that I saw the whole thing pass before my eyes in the instant of that blink."

There's something about Will's eyes. They seem burdened with the residue of a deeply impacted pain that over the years has been subsumed under the cloak of an imperturbable gaze. He appears reluctant to look me in the face for too long, though earlier he explained that this was part of his experience in the mines. Down in the shafts, because of the light on his helmet, he never looked another miner in the face for fear of blinding him.

"Nobody is more severe than Mother Nature. One time I was out with Ernie, and we watched a golden eagle pluck two crows out of the sky and drop them to the ground. Bam! he hit the first with his talons, and we watched him squeeze it to death as he was flying along. He circled around after he dropped the first and zoomed in and snatched another. Then he crushed that one and dropped it to the ground. He wasn't lookin' for something to eat. He was just practicin' how to kill.

"As kids we used to trap water snakes and stake them to ant hills. Sure we were cruel, but we didn't know any better. One time we caught a snake that had a big lump in its middle. We cut it open with a knife and out popped this frog and hopped away. I guess he couldn't have been in there too long. He was covered with slime, but he was still very much alive. Well, did we ever whoop and holler. Nature is full of surprises, I reckon. I once saw a water snake swallow its young to protect them from danger."

From 1983 to 1987, Will served in the navy. He'd lived in La Veta all his life, and he needed a change. He felt a curious urge to sail the ocean. He was a landlocked mountain boy transfixed by the spectacle of the open sea. He didn't mind sailing on ships wherever his duties took him, though to this day he remains wary of swimming.

I asked him about the bosun's mate tattoo on his right hand, at the fleshy part between the thumb and forefinger. "I just had to go to sea, though back then I didn't know why. I used to read a lot about Hugh Glass. Remember him? The guy who got mauled by a grizzly up in the Dakotas and was left to die by Jim Bridger and Tom Fitzpatrick, and who crawled on his belly for 200 miles to safety? Well, he was both a sailor and a mountain man. That always intrigued me. Now, I been both a sailor and a mountain man. So what was going on? One time, after I got out of the service, I found out why. Under a form of hypnosis I went back deep through my subconscious to the time in the 1830s and 1840s when, in an earlier life, I served as mate aboard a New Bedford whaling vessel. It got pretty scary I guess, 'cause during the session I kept using old-fashioned nautical terms that, even though I'd served in the navy, I had no way of knowing. At one point I told the therapist that I was scared of dying 'cause I'd seen the whale's eye when we were out one day trying to harpoon it. Well, if you saw the whale's eye it meant you were too close, and if it chose to it could swing its tail and smash your little boat to bits. So later in the session, I came to realize that I had in fact died at sea during this earlier life in a storm in the North Atlantic that sank my ship. Naturally, I was scared about reliving such an awful experience, but the therapist took me in slow and easy, and I saw myself clinging to a hatch cover in the dark as the sea swelled and raged. Then morning came, and I remember feeling the sun and thinking that I had somehow survived the night. But I was weak and exhausted, and I couldn't hold on any longer, and finally I let go and sank down and down into the depths of the sea."

Will stopped, his face thick with emotion. He looked down at his hands; then, seeming to gather himself, he went on. "The next thing I saw was my spirit—a white, shiny, ripply thing—shoot up to the surface and out into the sky."

He clenched and unclenched his right hand with its glistening bosun's tattoo. "When that therapist brought me out of it, I completely fell apart. I really opened up and let this stuff come out. It was the most traumatic experience I've ever gone through."

We sat in silence for a few minutes. Will seemed to have folded into himself like a sensitive plant at the onset of a storm. I wanted to keep him talking. "Tell me some more about La Veta," I said. "How has it changed since you were a kid?"

It took some effort for him to swivel his eyes around in my direction. Strange eyes, haunting, set in the mask of a formidable face, underslung with a solid, prognathous jaw.

"The question is how much to develop and where. During the past few years, so many of the old ranches like Goemmer's have been sold off. So when do you shut the door against any new development? Before the next guy gets here, or after he arrives? We don't have any industry to speak of here. There's very little farming or ranching left. Barely any lumbering. Virtually no mining. The traditional industries that occupied people's lives in this region are just about gone. True, there's some methane drilling west of here and over on the other side of Cuchara Pass. But now most everything is service-oriented. The Cuchara ski lodge employs maybe fifty or sixty people, though who knows how long it's going to stay open? La Veta is one of the poorest towns in one of the poorest counties in Colorado. Now if that's worth maintaining to preserve its small-town purity for the outsiders who like to visit, then I guess that's okay.

"There's too much play money floating around here these days. Money brought in by outsiders who made it somewhere else and now want to spend it so they can enjoy the sunsets and drive their SUVs without getting hung up in traffic. But the old ways of making a living are about shot. You don't see many high schoolers out bucking hay in the fields during the summers like I used to do. We always dealt with tourists, Texans and the like, who spent part of the summers with us and left their money to help tide us over. But they were just part of the scene, and they were always gone after Labor Day. Now we got these dot.commers from the big cities who can afford to live anywhere and work out of their homes on computers. Well, other than their money, what do they bring to the community? They're strangers here; they're totally fluid and mobile. They're like play people with lots of play money. Will they stick it out when the going gets tough? What's going to happen when the bear comes to these folks? When it shows up some night in their backyard, and they have to deal with it. You watch what happens to the bears in this town. We got four or five already, living in trees, eating out of garbage cans, knocking on people's doors. If we can live with them and not hurt them and not have them hurt us, well, maybe we'll be okay. I guess if we can live with the new breed of people moving in, then that's okay too. Give and take. Stuff coming from stuff. The way it's always been around here."

Profile Rock and Goemmer's Butte

Giants once roamed the area around the Spanish Peaks. They were quarrelsome and built rock walls behind which they took cover from the boulders they flung at one another. The earth shook and trembled from their exertions. The giants were haughty and proud, and they loved to make war.

The gods watched in despair as the fighting went on. Finally, they got angry and withheld rain from the area. When water became scarce, the giants called a truce and went in search of water. They left behind a lone warrior to stand guard over their beautiful valley.

The giants never came back. The solitary warrior remained steadfastly at his post. One day he sat down to rest, and the gods, taking pity on him, turned him into a stone monument for all to admire (Goemmer's Butte).

14
Riding With Anne Lucero
Along Trujillo Creek

You feel it as you drive up the valley from the town of Aguilar. Away from the interstate, away from the world of cell phones and crackling electronic devices. A soothing emotion steals over you that you can't really define. The valley is lovely to look at, filled with pastures and small fields and adobe dwellings tucked back under groves of trees; the farther you drive, the narrower it becomes. The twin peaks remain in view, looming to the north-northwest, rising tandem in double-headed profile or one at a time, depending on which way the dirt road forks and turns.

When you finally reach the house, perched on a shelf of land overlooking the road, you heave a sigh of relief. It's as if you've been here before, maybe not in actual fact but in your imagination, a secret reverie perhaps. It's the kind of place—cloistered, secluded, unspoiled—you've envisioned before. As you step from the car and bend down to let the pair of scruffy mutts sniff your fingers, you can't help but think that even if this is your first time out here, this place is where you belong. Maybe not every part of you because you're too disjointed to properly repose all your conflicted parts in a single place, but some part of you, some troubled part badly in need of succor and healing. A magpie garbles a fluty note from a nearby bush. The dogs growl in mock distress before retiring to the shade of the *portales* that runs along the south wall of the house. A hummingbird sips nectar from the spigot of a bright red feeder. Maybe you haven't been here before, but your visit, from the perspective of your frazzled, harried life, is long overdue.

Anne Lucero is a slim, attractive, fine-boned woman in her mid-seventies. She speaks with the precision and refinement of a schoolteacher, which she

Road to Anne Lucero's house outside Aguilar.

was in the valley for many years. Other than a couple of years spent in Denver during World War II, she has lived all her life along Trujillo Creek. She resides in a house originally built by her father in the early 1900s. The house is long and not very wide; it follows the dimensions of the narrow plot on which it sits. A steep hill rises in back, which prevents the house from expanding in that direction; new additions have been tacked on at either end rather than on top or in the middle. Out back, limited in size because of the hillside, there's a barn and a couple of sheds. In the old days, when Anne was growing up, the family farm was self-sufficient. "We didn't have to go to Aguilar to get anything for the longest time if we didn't want to," she tells me as we sit at her kitchen table with sunlight streaming through the rectangular window. "The valley was blessed with fertile black soil, and we grew corn, pumpkins, potatoes, beans, and squash. Twice a year we cleaned out the acequias. We had all the water we wanted from the creek or wells, and we had cattle and sheep. If we wanted a different kind of meat, we went hunting in the hills."

She paused, twining the petite fingers of both hands carefully together. "You asked about the bears back then. Well, we rarely saw them. That's because we knew where they lived, and they knew where we were. This was the last house at the head of the valley. Beyond this point, all the way to the

Grinding stone, Trujillo Creek.

Anne Lucero with background portraits of her parents, Dario Quintana and Fidelio Labe Quintana.

peaks, was pretty much wilderness. It wasn't like today, with people building all over the place, deep in the canyons, high on the ridges. We knew where we belonged, and so did they."

What is it about valleys that fosters a sense of serenity? Maybe it's the feeling of being snugly enfolded between protective ridges. Grassy pastures laced with flowing creeks. Cattle grazing between groves of apple trees. Contours and declivities that never become oppressive or confining. Anne Lucero has only to look down into the valley from her kitchen window or front door to know exactly where she belongs. These foothill valleys of the Spanish Peaks engender a delicate equipoise between mountain splendor and lowland modesty. Any day of the year, any hour of the day, Anne Lucero can glance out her window or front door and say what few of us can truthfully say at any time in our lives: "This is mine. This is where I belong. This is what I know better than any other place in the world."

But even paradise is fraught with peril. "When she was six, my sister was killed by a horse," Anne reveals. "She was riding on the back with a friend, on the way to school down in the valley, when some boys came up behind them and spooked the horse, and she fell off and the horse stepped on her skull. She died in a hospital in Trinidad."

Anne squints into the sunlight flooding through the south-facing kitchen window. "I never liked riding horses after that. My husband loved horses and always wanted me to ride with him. But I couldn't. I just couldn't."

After lunch, at Anne's suggestion, we took a slow, leisurely drive down the valley, back in the direction of the village of Aguilar, where Trujillo Creek flows into the Apishapa River. It was a brilliant day in late July. The sun beamed with radiant heat; the elevation of the valley at this point measures a little over 7,000 feet, and the air was pleasantly warm. The day before it had rained, settling the dust, permitting us to roll down the windows and drift along the graded dirt road like a canoe along a placid current. Anne pointed things out—a house, a grove of trees, a cluster of vines—and told stories about the early days in the valley. Her voice was quiet and refined; as she spoke, the string of words issuing from her lips seemed to become tangible, linking her to every object she identified.

At the site of the old Vigil homestead a mile or two down from her own, she pointed out a grove of elderberry trees standing close to where the house had been. Juan de Jesus Vigil brought his wife and family to Trujillo Creek in the 1860s. He built a big adobe house, which to Anne's dismay was torn down a few years ago. The family worked hard and eventually acquired sizable holdings in the valley. They cleared the land and cultivated it, they built homes and planted orchards, they grazed sheep and cattle.

"When the people first came, the valley was filled with trees," Anne said. "The soil was black and rich, and oh, how hard they worked to clear the trees so they could plant their fields! The work was dangerous, too. My grandfather, Blas Felipe Quintana, arrived at Trujillo Creek one summer in the 1870s. He and the family first stayed with the family of Juan de Jesus Vigil. One day Juan de Jesus and Blas Felipe rode through a forest which hadn't been homesteaded. They rode through stands of beautiful mariposa lilies which rose higher than their stirrups. Scarlet gilias and purple fleabane graced the sloping hillsides and creek banks. Occasionally, a clearing showed among the thick pines and ghostly aspens. Blas Felipe enjoyed the sound of the fluttering leaves. He told my grandmother about them, and they made plans to build a house amid those beautiful trees. Blas Felipe and his sons cleared the land of ponderosa, spruce, locust, and oak. They built an aspen cabin for their family. But sadly, while they were cutting the trees, Blas Felipe's oldest son, Ramon, was killed by a falling limb."

She paused and gazed out the car window. "You know, when someone died back then, even when I was growing up, a messenger on horseback went to each home in the community and left word of the death. The chapel bell tolled as the news spread through the valley. The neighbors gathered at the home of the bereaved to offer comfort and help. The men built a wooden coffin. The women bathed and prepared the body for burial. Seldom was a coroner called to verify the cause of death and embalm the body. The women did that. The people then came together for an all-night wake. They said prayers and sang *alabados*. At daylight, a team of black horses hitched to a wagon took the deceased to the cemetery. The entire community turned out for the burial."

There were no other vehicles on the road, so I downshifted into low gear, and the car chugged along at a turtle's pace while Anne spun forth more stories. The scent of ripe grass wafted through the open windows with a damp, fragrant odor. We crawled past a grove of mountain locust splashed with bright pink blossoms; messy magpie nests splotched the interior branches. A piñon jay sailed across the road. I spotted a rufous-sided towhee sporting in a patch of gambel oak.

In the late 1890s a two-room adobe schoolhouse was built halfway up the valley. At its peak, the school boasted seventy-five students. Attendance in all grades at one point increased so much that two teachers were hired. They earned fifty dollars a month and lived in a three-room cottage behind the school. They were responsible for keeping the place neat and tidy. Discipline was enforced with the flat of a yardstick. In winter, the older boys brought wood and coal to heat the stoves. They also helped carry drinking water from the nearest spring or well.

In 1939 the old two-room school was replaced by a bigger one built of native stone. "That's where I taught," Anne said, nodding at the square, yellowish lime-rock building as it came up on our left. "That's where I met my husband. It was at a wedding dance."

"Is it still a school?"

"No. It closed down in 1961. Today the kids are bused into Aguilar."

"How do you feel about that?"

"It makes me sad."

Mount Carmel Church, Trujillo Creek.

We slowed at the church, which rose off a knoll on the north side of the road. A belfry crowned the front wall above the door. The church was no longer in use, but despite that it appeared in good shape. Anne said it was built of adobe; in the 1940s a stucco exterior was added to retard the weathering of the mud bricks.

José Ramon Trujillo, after whom the creek is named, was the first Spanish pioneer to blaze a path through the valley. He came north with a surveying crew in the early 1860s. Ute Indians still camped in the valley, but José Ramon wasn't bothered by that. As an experienced farmer and rancher, he saw the potential the valley had as a new homeland for his family and friends. When he returned to Mora, New Mexico, he passed the word that in the north, over the line of the territory of Colorado, there was a place just waiting to be transformed into a blooming garden.

In the 1870s the first of these hardy settlers built a small chapel inside the walls of a *placita* located on top of a hill. By the end of the decade the community had grown so much it needed a new place of worship. Much discussion was devoted to where the chapel should be situated, how it would be built, and who would pay for the job. An adobe mason named Celedon Vigil molded three thousand adobe bricks. In addition, Vigil put his woodworking talents to use designing and carving the altar. For his efforts he was awarded an ox by the grateful community. The wet snows of March and April, coupled with the August monsoons, postponed completion of the project; two years later, on a fine summer day, the church, called Our Lady of Mount Carmel in honor of the order of the Carmelitas, a popular women's organization in the valley, was consecrated.

Like their male counterparts who belonged to the penitentes back in the time of Anne's youth, the Carmelitas were deeply religious. They led quiet, pious lives, placing themselves in thrall to the will of their husbands. Certain aspects of their lives they pledged to the Lady of Mount Carmel. They abstained from meat on Fridays. They fasted regularly and wore the brown Mount Carmel scapular around their necks. Frequently, they pinned Mount Carmel silver medals to their inner garments. A Carmelita woman never dressed in flamboyant colors, preferring muted blues, blacks, grays, and browns. The Carmelitas were the caretakers of the interior of the church. They donated beautiful linens for the altar. On July 16 they honored the Lady of Mount Carmel with a special ceremony. When a Carmelita languished near death, a container of sand or dirt was placed under her bed to remind her that she was about to return to the ground from which she had been formed.

"The old-style weddings were something to behold," Anne said in the car as we lingered in front of the church. "They were serious, of course, yet festive. The groom-to-be gave his parents the honor of asking for the hand of the young woman. The young woman's parents had to approve. If they did, they held an engagement party a few days before the wedding. The young man presented his bride-to-be with a ring. There was feasting and lively music. That's when, if all went well and there weren't too many feuds and animosities between them, the parents of the bride and groom began to call each other *compadre.* Following the engagement party, the bride's father took her shopping in Trinidad or Pueblo, where she bought some pretty clothes and maybe a piece of jewelry. This was the last time the father had to provide for her. After this, if she wanted something fancy, her husband had to buy it for her. The mother of the groom also took her son to buy clothes. In the future, his wife would help him select what he needed to wear.

"The wedding day was a joyous occasion. Following the religious ceremony, there was feasting, music, and dancing. The wedding dance took place either in Sanchez Hall or the schoolhouse. The dance always ended with the *entriega de novios,* or giving away. Before they got in the wagon and drove off, the couple was serenaded by an elaborate song strummed on a guitar and sung by a single person or sometimes by several people. The singers had rehearsed the song, and when they finished and the married couple rode away, the festivity was over and the young people were on their own."

Our final stop that afternoon was the Trujillo Creek Cemetery. It lies on a slope of land on the north side of the road. Many of the early Hispanic

Cerquita, Trujillo Creek Cemetery.

pioneers are buried there. Not even Anne knows for certain how old it is or who was the first to be buried there. Next to the gate there's a milpa that nourishes a few anemic stalks of corn, presided over by a scarecrow decked out in a faded polka-dot shirt and battered straw hat.

Inside the cemetery we got out of the car and strolled between the headstones. A few of the older graves were marked by wooden crosses or lichen-covered slabs with the dates and lettering practically weathered away. Individual plots were decorated with sprays of artificial flowers, which added a touch of color to the drab grass that grew everywhere in spiky tufts. One or two of the older graves were enclosed by a *cerquita,* a rectangular boundary of worn and faded sticks pointed at the tips like a picket fence. Anne showed me the gravesite of her parents and grandparents. "We used to take better care of the cemetery than we do now," she said, a note of fretfulness sounding between the careful punctuality of her speech. "But once a year, in spring, we organize a cleanup. People from as far away as Denver who have relatives here sometimes show up. My ancestors are buried here, and this is where I will lie when my time comes."

She looked at me, her face a curious mix of acceptance, resignation, and profound contentment. "Where else could I possibly go? Where else do I belong?"

The Gods of Huajatolla

The Rain God once lived on the heights of Huajatolla. In his workshop he shaped the clouds and sent them sailing over the world to nourish the plants and animals with summer rains. The name of the Rain God was Tlaloc. When he failed to send down rain, it was because he was angry and upset. Beautiful girls were then sacrificed at the Sacred Well to placate Tlaloc.

The Sun God also lived on Huajatolla. He, too, was a source of life, a provider. He invigorated the lives of the people with the brightness of day. He made the bears wake up in spring and scratch their bellies. He warmed the crops in the fields and helped them grow.

Other gods lived on the heights of Huajatolla. The Thunder Gods battled between themselves with giant boulders. The whole world reverberated with the sound of their conflict. The huge rocks at the foot of the double mountain were their weapons, and the giant stone walls that run down the sides, called the Walls of Cuchara, were the breastworks behind which they took cover.

15
Among the Penitentes

We know the popular version, the one that's been stereotyped for hundreds of years. A line of somberly dressed men emerges from a windowless, one-story adobe structure and marches up a muddy lane splotched with patches of melted snow. In the lead plods a *rezador* who intones the words of a soulful prayer recounting Christ's suffering that terrible last day of His mortal life. A stooped figure playing a *pito,* or homemade reed flute, follows the *rezador,* piping a melancholy trill that fills the April air with a mournful lament. Behind the *pitero* come the flagellants, stripped to the waist, their faces twisted with pain, who scourge themselves with the sinewy tentacles of a multi-tipped whip expressly to experience a measure of the grief Christ endured as He hung from the cross. At the end of the line a man drags a wooden cross, heavy and cumbersome, that will be propped upright in the ground at a secret *calvario,* perhaps with the man lashed to it, in emulation of the manner in which Jesus Christ was affixed to the post that for two millennia has come to represent His agony and His redemption.

"The idea of the whip as a means of grace is one of the oldest in the history of nations," wrote Charles Lummis, an early Anglo observer of native customs in the Southwest. "Herodotus tells us that the ancient Egyptians flogged themselves in honor of Isis. The boys of Sparta were whipped before the altar of Artemis Orthia. In the Roman Lupercalia devout citizens esteemed it a felicity to be struck by the leathern thongs of the Luperci. And by the beginning of the fifth century the Christian church came to recognize the virtues of the lash for offending monks" (Lummis, p. 57).

No sect or organization in the Southwest has stirred as much controversy as the order of Los Hermanos Penitentes. Its origin is obscure. The order was founded in Spain around four hundred years ago. Initially, it had nothing of the lash about it. The members—"men of good morals and good sense" (Lummis, p. 58)—met for religious study and discussion. The prototype of the order was brought to Mexico, and later to what is now New Mexico and southern Colorado, by Franciscan friars in the company of Spanish conquistadors. The first recorded bout of public self-flagellation occurred in 1598 when Don Juan de Oñate, leading a party northward to colonize New Mexico, scourged himself in a private act of contrition on Good Friday amid the dreary sound of doleful chanting by Franciscan friars clothed in girdles fashioned from cactus thorns. One historical account fairly revels in the deed: "The night was one of prayer and penance for all. The soldiers with cruel scourges beat their backs unmercifully until the camp ran crimson with their blood" (Simmons, *Last Conquistador,* p. 98).

The brotherhood expanded over the next three centuries as the influence of the Franciscans declined. First under Spanish rule, then under Mexico—for complicated political reasons—Franciscan friars were forced to leave the country. With the U.S. acquisition of Spanish lands north of the Rio Grande in 1848, penitentes in some communities stepped in to fill the void left by the absence of a viable clergy.

Historians trace the rise of the order in the nineteenth century to several possible antecedents. When Spanish conquistadors first entered New Mexico, they found evidence of blood sacrifice among the Indians whose pueblos they subjugated along the Rio Grande Valley. Additionally, members of the order may have been influenced by a sect of medieval *flagellanti* initiated in the thirteenth century by Saint Anthony of Padua. Religious plays put on by traveling companies enacted Christ's suffering on the cross and brought the message of His life to people in remote areas of the New World. Another influence was the Rule of the Third Order that Saint Francis of Assisi established in the thirteenth century, which touted a life of simplicity, humility, and piety.

The exact origin of Los Hermanos Penitentes will probably never be sufficiently explained. But as scholar Marta Weigle has said, "Whatever their beginnings, the Penitente Brotherhoods are clearly not aberrant. They exist well within the history of Spanish Catholicism and its mystical, penitential, and Franciscan traditions. Maintained by colonists in a hostile frontier with a climate similar to their Spanish homeland, it is not at all surprising that this is so" (Weigle, p. 13).

William Roybal is an elderly man well into his seventies with a charming smile and gentle manner. I met him and his wife, Trinidad, one afternoon in late September in a convenience store in the little town of Avondale, located on the Arkansas River, twenty miles east of Pueblo. Through a miscommunication we had trouble making connection, and as he shook my hand in a shy, tentative fashion, he apologized for the delay. He was a short man, compact, rather dapper in a striped button-down shirt and khaki jacket. His teeth glowed like polished bone. He laughed easily, and

the corners of his eyes were splashed with a myriad of crinkles. Roybal is a penitente, one of the few remaining, by his estimate, in the Spanish Peaks region. He had agreed, along with Trinidad, to meet with Barbara Sparks and myself and show us the church and other facilities where the brotherhood conducts its services during the Lenten season. We followed them in our car along a dirt road that led out of Avondale, south along the steep cut banks of the lower Huerfano River. The road soon lost its rural width and became little more than a dirt track snaking south-southwest across open grassland, with the Spanish Peaks clearly in view 60 miles away. The land had obviously been overgrazed in the past; arroyos cut deep furrows across the flat surface, and the dry grass was spiked with prickly cholla. Tufts of rabbitbrush, tinged a mournful yellow, flashed along both sides of the dirt track. In the distance we discerned a compound of three buildings rising out of the unruly grass, backlit by the afternoon sun, which threw their outlines into shadowy relief. Bill got out of his car and opened a gate. A moment later we bumped inside, pulling up near the entrance to a long, rectangular, west-facing church.

It was cool inside the church, soothing and quiet. The ceiling was painted blue, the altar bare and unadorned. "We used to keep our santos here," Bill said, "but no more. Vandals have trashed us too many times.

Huerfano Church and *morada* with Chinese elm.

Trinidad and William Roybal,
Huerfano Church.

One time they threw the pews through the windows, and we found them
piled up outside in a mess of broken glass. But we put it back together, and
we'll keep putting it back together no matter how many times they return."

Both Bill and Trinidad radiate an aura of unflappable civility and strength.
Trinidad told us how she came from a penitente family in the region and
what the Easter season was like when she was a little girl. "My grandfather
helped build this church in the 1890s. He was a member of the order and
remained so until he died. We used to come and spend all of Holy Week
here, my entire family—cousins, aunts, uncles, nieces, nephews—as well
as friends. Oh, there were many in the brotherhood back then, and we
took over the *deposito,* and the women cooked meals on a wood stove, and
I helped in any way a small girl could help. For that week we lived humbly
and well. Neither my grandfather or father would allow the place to be
wired for electricity, and so we made do with kerosene lamps and by cooling our perishables in the cistern. Those were wonderful times, so peaceful
and holy. For a week at least of every year we lived in genuine harmony
with God and each other."

Bill Roybal looked fondly at his wife. "We observed a round-the-clock
vigil for the entire week," he added. "We're too old to do that now, and there
just aren't that many of us left anymore. Back then we had a *mayordomo,* not a
brother, who orchestrated everything and made sure we did what we had to do

Deposito, Holy Week, Huerfano Church.

on time. At the height of our power, there were as many as thirty or forty penitentes on the premises. Day and night, we had at least twelve singing and twelve praying and twelve eating over in the *deposito* so they could continue with the singing and praying when the others got tired or hungry."

We stepped outside the church into the windless air. I tried to imagine what the place must have looked like with all those people generating worshipful thoughts, how it must have felt, the ambiance it must have given off. Bill then escorted us to the *morada* and opened the door. The *morada* was low and squat, consisting of three rooms; one, a storage room, he didn't open. The walls were painted a pale green. The middle room was bare and sparsely furnished. The chapel where the brothers prayed and made their devotions was similarly bare; a couple of *retablos* hung on the walls. I flashed back to the *morada* Floyd Chavez had showed us the previous Easter, tucked away at the edge of a private road outside the town of Weston on the south slope of the Spanish Peaks. The *morada* had been abandoned for many years, and the owner of the property on which it sat had used it to shelter his cattle. In one room there was a stone fireplace where the penitentes did their cooking. The floor of the windowless room where the brothers did their scourging was littered with generations of cow piles. The adobe walls were splotched with unsavory marks. Blood, I thought, and asked Floyd, who shrugged. "We were kids," he said. "We used to hide in the woods

Altar, Holy Week, Huerfano
Church.

across the road and watch them when they came out carrying the big cross. We'd follow them a little ways up the road, but never to where it was they put the cross in the ground. It was too scary. My father would have smacked me good if he knew I was spying on them."

Another flashback filled my thoughts as we stood outside the *morada* with Bill and Trinidad. Good Friday, 1971 or 1972. I had driven with a friend from Ojo Caliente, New Mexico, to Truchas, a mountain town on the road between Española and Taos. We were in a store on the main drag watching a rug maker work her loom when suddenly we heard something in the street. I stepped to the door in time to watch a line of somberly dressed men climb out of a gully in back of the stores on our side of the street. Unhurried, in single file, led by two men, one holding a small cross, the other a fluttering banner, they crossed the street at a solemn ceremonial pace. Traffic ground to a halt; pedestrians on the sidewalk, Anglo and Hispanic, paused to watch. I think I remember hearing the reedy quaver of a wooden flute. The men in the procession could have been marching on the face of the moon for all the awareness they had of the people watching them. Their gloomy faces looked inexpressibly sad. Their feet touched the same ground as ours, but they clearly belonged to another realm. There may have been fifteen or twenty of them. They filed across the street and

Chavez brothers, Holy Week, in procession to *morada*.

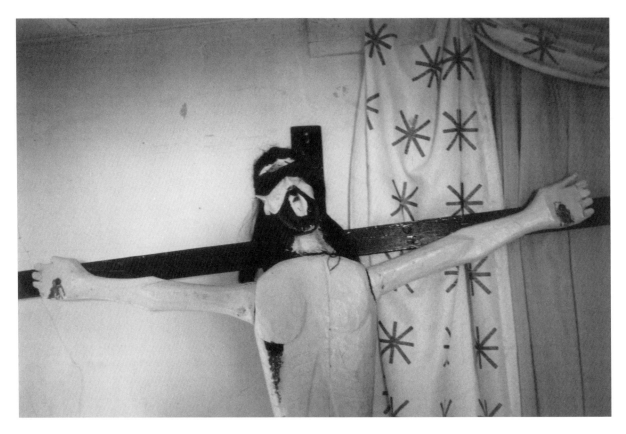

Deposito interior, Good Friday, santo of Jesus Christ.

proceeded down an alley between two buildings and disappeared through a gate into somebody's backyard.

Following our tour of the *morada* Bill and Trinidad took us through the *deposito,* a roomy one-story building located at the west edge of the compound. In back was a kitchen with cupboards and a wood stove; in front, a spacious parlor with couches, tables, and chairs. The walls were painted the same soft green as the walls of the interior of the *morada.* This is where the women prepared food, where it was served, where people sang hymns and held prayer services. The prohibition on electric appliances is still enforced by Bill and Trinidad. "We keep it that way so people can go into the past whenever they want to," Trinidad said. "It just seems fitting and proper."

"We used to do the Stations of the Cross outside in the yard," said Bill. "But we've gotten so old and so many of us use walkers and crutches, we hold it inside the big room here."

Outside the east door, between the *deposito* and the church, stood an old China elm, forlorn and solitary, its gnarled limbs creaking in the light, dry wind. The tree was tall and messy with splintered branches, shorn of all leaves but a transparent, papery few.

Trinidad's face suffused with a special brightness as she reminisced about the old days. "We don't have the same depth of faith anymore," she said. "My father went on his knees all the way from the church to the altar inside the *deposito.* A hundred yards, would you say? He went the entire distance carrying a boy child. Not a girl. A boy. We girls walked ahead of him side by side. My father believed the girls would be taken care of by whoever they married. After all, that was the way it was. That was the way it had always been. But the boys—the boys needed all the faith and strength they could get."

"It's always been hard to be a penitente," Bill confessed. A sad expression stole over his face. "We've endured a lot of persecution, not just from Anglos but from Hispanics who think we're different and strange. It began when we left the safety of the family home and went off to school. We got teased on the playground. During Easter, kids threw rocks at us. And all because we choose to experience Christ's suffering in a more intimate and personal way."

He sighed. "I think all the trouble in the world stems from people having no respect for other people's beliefs."

"Some kids once asked our children if it was true that we sacrificed a baby at Easter time," Trinidad said. "Can you imagine that? Penitentes only wish to go through Holy Week undisturbed. Holy Week for them is a constant exercise of prayer."

A generous smile rumpled her smooth face. She clutched a batch of manzanilla and explained to Barbara and me how to brew it into a refreshing tea. Trinidad's grandmother was a *curandera,* and she herself was well versed in local *remedios.* "People came for miles to talk to my grandmother. She would rub an egg across the belly of a colicky child, and where the egg broke was the spot where the child hurt the most. All the time she prayed. That's what made her so good. The *remedios* won't work without prayer. She did everything with prayer."

Back in the car, bumping over lumpy, dry ground. The Spanish Peaks appear in the distance, shapely forms of alluring beauty floating on a cushion of blurry, late afternoon air. We follow Bill and Trinidad on a side track a short ways to a wild, tangled patch of sage, wheat grass, and yucca. Inside another wire gate we see a few headstones scattered about. Tall, crinkly sunflowers bob in the soft breeze. I read the headstones on a few random graves, which turn out to be Trinidad's parents. Fidel Gomez 1893–1975. Andrea Gomez 1910–1984.

Side by side, Bill and Trinidad crunch across the dry, starchy grass to an empty plot next to Trinidad's parents. The wind flutters teasingly past my shoulder. To the east, the flatlands unfurl like a wide, nappy carpet. The tough, springy forbs and grasses appear on the verge of concealing all traces of the people who've been laid to rest here. Trinidad looks down at the stony plot at her feet. "This is where we'll lie when our time comes," she says.

"It's comforting to know this is where you'll be for eternity," Bill echoes. "It's part of our Easter service to offer *sudarios* to the souls of the departed. That way we keep them fresh in our hearts and minds. That way it all stays connected."

The Evil Priest

When Coronado returned to Mexico after searching for Quivera in the 1540s, he left behind three monks who wished to bring the message of God to the natives. Two of the monks tried to teach Christianity to the Indians, and both were martyred for their efforts. The third monk, Juan de la Cruz, claimed to have subdued the demons of the twin mountains, placed there by the gods to prevent anyone from taking out any silver or gold. Using local Indians as slaves, Father de la Cruz extracted a staggering amount of wealth. After the Indians had served their purpose, he put them to the sword. He and his cohorts then loaded their pack animals with glinting nuggets and bars and disappeared by devious routes into Mexico. They were never seen again.

16
John Ritter

Few things are more revealing than history observed close-up by a partici-
pant. Gail Ritter, third-generation proprietor of the Ritter Ranch, located
outside La Veta, has seven letters written by her grandfather, John Ritter,
dating between 1865 and 1880, detailing his hopes, dreams, and aspira-
tions. The letters offer an intimate glimpse not only of Ritter's personal life
but of early ranching days in the Spanish Peaks.

John Ritter was born in Hickorytown, Pennsylvania, in 1836. He was
the great-great-grandson of Paul and Elizabeth Ritter, who immigrated from
Germany to America in 1732. John Ritter served in the Union cavalry
during the Civil War and saw action at Gettysburg. "How much action we
never knew," says Gail Ritter. "He never spoke about it."

By early 1865 it was evident that John Ritter was disenchanted with the
military. In the first of a series of letters he wrote to his cousin Jacob
Stauffer, he encouraged the younger man not to enlist but to remain in
school until spring. "That would be better than going as a drummer boy,"
he declared. As for his own plans, he spoke vaguely about heading out
West.

But he didn't go right away. After being mustered out of the service, he
traveled around his native state checking out employment opportunities. In
a letter to Jacob Stauffer's father ("Friend Uncle") dated July 22, 1865, he
says that oil has been discovered in the town of Titusville, and the place is
booming. Over three hundred new houses have been built; his uncle was a
tinsmith and owned a stove company, and young Ritter felt that Titusville
might be a good place for him to invest his time and money. He then
speaks enthusiastically about forming a company and leasing some land

and drilling for oil. "I will risk $300," he tells his uncle—a considerable amount of money for the time. Reading between the lines, it's apparent that he wants his uncle to invest with him; the letter is a not too subtle appeal from a young man just getting started to an older, more established figure for whatever help he can extend. Evidently, young John didn't get on too well with his biological father, and he turned to his uncle as a surrogate. "There is money to be made in this country," he declares.

The proposed oil deal never materialized, for Ritter's next letter to his cousin is dated February 9, 1868. While ideas for making money may have been easy to concoct, actual coin was hard to come by, and to get out West John Ritter was forced to reenlist in the cavalry. He served for a couple of years and left the service, most likely at Fort Union in New Mexico Territory. In this letter, written from Ute Creek, near Elizabethtown, Ritter confesses that things are not going too well. The winter's been long and hard, with much snow. Gold has been discovered in the area of Ute Creek, which legally forms part of the extensive Maxwell Land Grant, and people are starting to pour in from all over the country. Again, Ritter counsels his cousin to remain in school. New Mexico, he says, "is a hard country, dam poor living, no vegetables of any kind." He then adds, "I wish I was back in old Norristown long enough to get a square meal or two."

Three months later, on May 10, 1868, Ritter tells his cousin that people are rushing into the area by the hundreds. The women are Mexican, and their men are very jealous. He tells Jacob that it would cost him about $300 to come west; he then advises him to wait a couple of years until the railroad is completed. He also advises him to learn "the Mexican language." To travel through this country, he says, "you want a pony to ride and a mule to pack and a pair of revolvers strapped to your side and a big Bowie knife."

It's apparent that things haven't gone too well for John Ritter. He has ideas aplenty and the energy to float them, but he can't quite link the two together in a lucrative fashion. Like other veterans of the Civil War, he's ready to take advantage of the peace and prosperity he fought to preserve; but the dream of striking it rich—even of making a decent living—has so far eluded him. Whatever scheme he had in mind for drilling oil or selling stoves in his native Pennsylvania had evidently come to naught. He apparently tried his hand at gold mining during the 1868 boom in New Mexico, with no significant results.

Three years later we find him homesteading along the Cuchara River in the Spanish Peaks. In a letter dated September 11, 1871, he tells his cousin that the late-summer weather produced heavy rains, which resulted in lots of good grass and a fine hay crop. He announces delightedly that "we are getting lots of girls out here, and some pretty nice ones." Many of them are from Georgia, and his only complaint is that "they use snuff and tobacco." The last three years have seen a huge influx of settlers to the region. He says he wants to get married; at the same time he wants to go back to Pennsylvania. "Jake," he concludes, "this is mighty healthy country and I

Original John Ritter homestead,
built in 1889, La Veta.

hate to leave it." He laments that he hasn't heard from his father or brothers for two years. He knows there's money to be made in the cattle business; even if they aren't fed during the winter, they still "come out fat in the spring just from the grass." That evidently strikes a responsive chord, and he closes by saying that next spring he intends to go to Mexico to purchase a young herd.

The last letter (February 27, 1880) is written from a homestead along the Cuchara River, several miles northeast of present-day Walsenburg. He tells Jacob that his brother Kim has joined him. (Kim homesteaded a 160-acre parcel adjoining his own.) Together they have "made some fence"—strung barbwire across their land—which, multiplied a thousandfold throughout the region, was to spell the end of the open range and contribute to the demise of huge enterprises such as the British-owned Prairie Cattle Company. At age forty-four, Ritter admits he has "been trying to get me an old woman." The previous summer he branded 150 calves and three colts, a clear indication that after all these years he has found his true vocation. The forthcoming summer he hopes to increase his stock to 200 calves and six to eight colts. "When spring opens," he says confidently, "times will be good." He concedes that prospecting for gold and silver has become a tempting pursuit but that it's a young man's game, implying that he's too old to try it himself. "There have been big changes in this country the last five years," he concludes, "and there will be bigger the next five."

The American dream of a more rewarding life was proving elusive for John Ritter. All around him in the region of the Spanish Peaks, countless other men were engaged in the same quest for material success. They'd known hard times and would continue to know them; there seemed no magic formula or quick fix that would enable him to realize the dreams that had compelled him to abandon his native Pennsylvania for a life out on the harsh frontier. Despite the genuine success with cattle he had achieved, he still thought about selling out and going to New Mexico or California. "I like this business," he confesses to his cousin, "but the country is becoming too crowded. And the sheep are ruining it."

Less than a month after he wrote this final letter to his cousin, John Ritter married Julietta Beatrice Watson McFarland, a widow with three children, in Greenhorn, Colorado. Together they would have eight more children, including Kimery Ernest Ritter, Gail Ritter's father. (Gail Ritter says that when her grandmother would tell her grandfather that they were going to have another child, he would shrug and say, "Another sack of flour, another pair of shoes.")

Kimery Ritter was born in 1889 in a log cabin (still standing), located on a rambling piece of property purchased by John Ritter the year before. The spread followed the meandering curves of the Cuchara River downstream from the town of La Veta, near the point where the foothills of the great double peaks commence to rumple out onto the plains.

John Ritter may not have tapped into the same dazzling bonanza the Rockefeller family did during the Titusville oil boom, but he did lay the foundation for a solid ranching establishment. When he died in 1924, the ranch had expanded to a thousand acres, supporting sheep as well as cattle. Many ranchers of the era were cash poor but land rich; the cattle and sheep they ran were as good as greenbacks or gold coins. Liquidity, or the lack thereof, would become a burning issue in the last decades of the nineteenth century, especially in the agrarian West and South. The panic of 1873 collapsed banks and tightened credit all over the nation; it wasn't unusual for a cattleman to drive a few head into Trinidad or Walsenburg or La Veta and trade them for food and supplies. Frank Bloom, who built the Bloom House in Trinidad and whose Bloom Cattle Company eventually extended from New Mexico to Montana, always maintained he backed into the business by accepting cows as payment for merchandise from his store in Trinidad.

Liquid or not, John Ritter had come a long way from Gettysburg to this scenic location at the foot of the Spanish Peaks. Each generation of the rural West measures its self-worth by an evolving standard, but the basis for any final determination of monetary or emotional value lies in the land. Viewed today, shorn of the threat of Indians, rustlers, grasshoppers, and economic depressions, the Ritter Ranch seems positively edenic. Few locations west of the hundredth meridian can match it for sheer pastoral beauty.

Gail Ritter in front of original homestead.

But beauty resides in the eye of the beholder, and it's unlikely that John Ritter, with all the work he had to do, had much time for the scenic aspects of the place he acquired in 1888. With eleven children and several hundred head of sheep and cattle to manage, his perception of the property was necessarily utilitarian. How can I work this land so that it will produce enough food to keep us all alive and well? he must have asked himself.

One generation's meal ticket is another's aesthetic treasure; today, on both sides of the peaks, old ranches are being sold off and carved up into 35-acre "ranchettes," eagerly sought by jaded urbanites anxious to escape the crush of cities and live in a place where the echoes of a meaningful past seem palpably evident. For such dreamers the Ritter Ranch presents a perfect location, but third-generation owner Gail Ritter will have nothing to do with it. In the summer of 1999 she placed the entire property in a conservation easement, which legally bars "forever" its use for real estate or other commercial development. "A few years ago I dreamed I saw bulldozers rolling across the ranch, clearing the lush pasture for a huge housing development," she says. "I woke up in a cold sweat and called my lawyer and began figuring out a way to prevent this from ever happening."

Walking the ranch one December morning, trodding the dry grass, inspecting the original log cabin, pens, sheds, and other outbuildings,

One-hundred-year-old fence,
Ritter Ranch.

listening to the wind rattle the few leaves still clinging to the ancient cotton-woods towering over the yard, it's easy to understand why. This place is the real thing, the beau ideal of the historical West, an authentic ranch built by authentic pioneers back in a time when human beings measured their accomplishments by the yardstick of their senses. The Ritter Ranch preserves in ambient glory the relics of another era. Time and the elements have weathered these relics to the warp and curve of genuine artifacts. Hallowed by decades of human use, these artifacts embody the distillation of an entire cultural ethos in their simple, functional lines. You can understand why the concepts of honor and integrity were so important to people like John Ritter. You can see it in the bend and shape of the implements he used, the way form dovetails effortlessly with function, the mix of pride and humility that suffuses the face of Gail Ritter as she points these things out to visitors.

Take the barn, for example. Built in 1907, it's the cathedral of out-buildings on the ranch. It's tall with a peaked roof, modeled on the Pennsylvania Dutch barns of John Ritter's native state. The sides are marked with shutters, doors, the odd window or two. It looks supremely functional yet feels utterly personal, stamped by the hands and minds of the people who designed and constructed it. A creaky half door on the east side opens onto

Adobe barn, Ritter Ranch.

a rough-hewn plank floor strewn with wisps of straw. The walls are grounded by slabs of native sandstone; adobe bricks, flecked with tawny chaff, soar to the top of the steeply pitched ceiling. Thick posts and solid crossbeams provide interior support. Somewhere up there, pigeons gurgle and flutter amid a fallout of loose feathers. The wind seeps through the warped planks of a tiny cupola perched atop the angled roof, presaging a change in the weather. The barn seems more organic than structural, a living, breathing entity, decaying in situ one slow, steady tick at a time. Other than a few coils of wire, a few tools and hooks, there's nothing synthetic or manufactured in the place. Bits and strands of detritus—part straw, part animal hair, part insect residue—cling to the posts and crossbeams. Outside, deer tracks congeal in a patch of frozen mud. The leafless limbs of the box elders edging the fence between the barn and the house shiver and creak in the rising wind.

There's nothing electronic here, nothing furtive or unseen; the barn and everything in it represent the old world of tactile sensations, the immediate and tangible world of our grandparents. This world—concrete, objective, and measurable—provided the moral and emotional underpinnings that enabled them to endure what they had to endure, both personally and on a global scale.

Interior, adobe barn, Ritter Ranch.

Consider the Great Depression, which, coupled with a terrible drought, devastated the ranching industry in the Spanish Peaks. Those homesteaders with at least 320 acres tried to hang on, but the wind blew incessantly; decades of irresponsible plowing and grazing had decimated the grass and topsoil, and it blew away in dark, rolling clouds that cast a pall upon the land. Starving livestock roamed the range looking for edible grass. In 1934 the federal government inaugurated a program whereby it paid owners thirteen dollars a head to round up their starving cattle and shoot them. Experienced ranchers were hard put to hold on, and most were forced to borrow heavily to buy feed to maintain their dwindling herds. Bankers were caught in a bind; as the collateral value of land and cattle declined, so did their willingness to make loans. It was a bleak time in the history of the Spanish Peaks. Gail Ritter remembers her parents going to town with less than a couple of dollars in their pockets. "If they had a penny left over to buy a postage stamp to mail a letter, they did so. If they didn't have that extra penny, the letter was left unmailed."

Purgatoire River

In 1594 the two leaders of a Spanish expedition, having failed to find gold along the banks of a river flowing out from the foothills of the twin peaks, dissolved into rancorous quarreling. Eventually, Juan Hermana killed Francisco Bonilla and became the jefe of the group. The priest who accompanied them refused to follow a murderer and, leading a contingent of defectors, returned to Mexico. Hermana and the others forged ahead, obsessed with finding gold. They were never seen again, but their bones and armor were later discovered along the river. Apparently, they were ambushed by Indians and perished to a man. Since they died without benefit of last rites, they were said to be in Purgatory, and the river was named "El Rio de Las Animas Perdidas en Purgatorio" (the River of Souls Lost in Purgatory).

French explorers later shortened the name to La Purgatoire (Pur-ga-twa). Anglos called it "Picketwire."

17
Down in Picketwire Canyon

It's early June, a blistering day, and I'm down in Picketwire Canyon, strolling along the trail leading to the dinosaur track site, a distance of 5.3 miles according to the interpretive material I picked up at the Comanche National Grasslands Visitor Center in La Junta. It's midmorning by the time I come down off the flats into the surprisingly ample depths of this secretive canyon, located far out on the plains. The Picketwire, or Purgatoire, or Purgatory River issues from the Culebra Range of the Sangre de Cristo Mountains. It splashes down through the southerly foothills of the Spanish Peaks, through the gap in the Dakota Wall at the hamlet of Stonewall, past the abandoned facilities of the Allen coal mine, past the site of the San Ysidro Church, past Floyd Chavez's spread near the village of Weston, through the town of Trinidad (pop. 11,000), out onto the flats in a north-easterly direction toward a confluence with the Arkansas east of La Junta.

It's been a wet spring; several snows fell in April on the Spanish Peaks, and the runoff everywhere has been vigorous. The glimpses I get of the Purgatoire as I inch my way down the steep trail indicate that it's flowing at a brisk pace. In a month or so the current will falter and slow, and the cut bed through which the water now purls will barely glimmer with a few damp patches.

It's another world down here, cloistered and protected; the wind barely blows, and the heat stacks high in palpable layers. There are so many more plants, flowers, and trees down here than up on the flats. Groves of willows and cottonwoods flourish at intervals. Long, grassy ledges of prime grazing land extend above the steep river banks, which the U.S. Forest Service (of which the national grasslands are a branch) leases to ranchers for a minimal fee. The dry climate down in these depths cures the grass on the ground, which conserves their nutritive value through the fall and winter, enabling cattle to forage off them long after the grass on top has dried up and blown away. Today, these grasses are splashed with colorful wildflowers. I dutifully list them in my little notebook (though with diminishing enthusiasm as the long hike unfolds)—yellow flax, lupine, mariposa, Indian paintbrush, white evening primrose, spiderwort . . .

Traditionally in the spring, Comanche, Cheyenne, and Kiowa warriors fattened their horses on the early grass growing along the rivers down in sheltered canyons such as the Picketwire. The broad benches offered a diverse sampling of eastern and western flora: buffalo and grama grass, low shrubs, different kinds of forbs, big and little bluestem, side-oats grama. The eastern grasses sprouted in early March. Weak from hunger, both horses and bison built up their strength by grazing along these rivers. In late spring and early summer the animals moved up to the highlands between the streams to take advantage of the short grasses, which greened out later to avoid the killing blow of an unexpected spring storm. These short grasses weren't nearly as lush as the river cover, but by early June they were at their peak potency, and the sloping divides between the watercourses were transformed into succulent pastures.

Driving south from La Junta across the undulant surface of the plains, Picketwire Canyon comes as a complete surprise. There's no warning it's even there; you turn off the graveled county road onto a private track, rumble past a corral and water tank, ride up and down over several rises, and suddenly you're at the edge of a wide fissure that splits the dry, grassy surface like a tear in a canvas sheet. Masses of piñon and juniper screen the rim; it's down through this minty, fragrant forest that you proceed, along a narrow rock-strewn trail that slants precipitously to the canyon floor. The air down there is dry. It chaps your membranes and squeezes the moisture from the back of your throat. It's laced with dust and bits of airborne grass. Spiky growths of yucca and prickly pear sprout amid swales of mixed grasses. Once upon a time it was a lot wetter, a few thousand years ago in the wake of the retreating glaciers, when there were spruce forests and marshy wetlands and huge, hairy creatures stalked by fur-clad hunters bearing atlatls and stone-tipped spears. But the last century and a half of settlement have taken their toll, and the land, even in this secluded fold, looks a bit threadbare and scrubby.

Despite these signs, the ribbony width of the river valley nurtures a wider variety of birds and flora than up on the flats. Early pioneers followed the watercourses that etch the surface of the Great Plains west of the greeny folds of the Ozark Plateau and Missouri River Valley, taking advantage of the timber, water, and grass that grew in these protected areas. The rivers carve shallow channels out of the friable surface of the plains, sometimes to the depth of little more than a ditch, sometimes, as in the Picketwire, down several hundred feet. They form natural corridors along which birds and animals and plant life drift and roam, inching far upriver from their natural habitats east of the hundredth meridian into the inhospitable aridity of the High Plains. Early inhabitants used the canyons in a similar manner, not only as a source of water and wood but to winter in, away from drifting snow and howling winds.

The potential was there from the beginning. Pioneer ranchers in the Spanish Peaks region such as John Prowers brought in a few head of cattle in the 1860s to graze along the Arkansas River, east of the mouth of the Purgatoire. He observed the miles and miles of rolling grass and saw a future that held no place for buffalo. Cattle were in demand back East to feed a growing population, swelled by the seemingly inexhaustible influx of European immigrants. By 1865 the Chicago stockyards were in full swing; by 1870 the refrigerated rail car appeared; a decade later, once the railroad linked La Veta, Walsenburg, and Trinidad, it was possible to ship all kinds of meat by rail, whether on hoof or carcasses. A simple statistic tells it all: in 1860 there were no recorded cattle in the state of Colorado; twenty years later there were 1.8 million.

The shelter and grass drew ranchers like Charles Goodnight to the canyons of the Apishapa and Picketwire. The land was good and there was lots of it, which enabled them to prosper in a relatively short time. Perhaps the most notable ranch in the region was the J. J. Cattle Company, established in 1869 by James C. Jones and his brothers Peyton and Stephen. In 1881 they sold the operation to the British-owned Prairie Cattle Company for $625,000. The sale included 55,000 cattle, 300 horses, and over 2 million acres of land. Because the land was virtually unfenced, cattle roamed on rangeland stretching from the Arkansas River to the New Mexico border.

Under the energetic leadership of Murdo McKenzie, the Prairie Cattle Company grew in size to over 5 million acres and 140,000 head of cattle, which made it the biggest cattle company in the world at that time, with extensive holdings in Colorado, Texas, and the Oklahoma panhandle. In Colorado the company continued to use the J. J. brand. McKenzie, a ruddy-faced Scotsman, traveled in a private railroad car accoutered with plush accessories, accompanied by his personal valet and chef. He dressed impeccably in the latest fashion, replete with top hat, silk cravat, and pearl stickpin. He looked every bit the part of the corporate cattle baron, as different from the rustic demeanor of the homespun Charles Goodnight as can be imagined.

Access to and control over water was essential to these big companies, as well as to the smaller ranches and homesteads that began to dot the Spanish Peaks countryside in the 1880s and 1890s. When the Prairie Cattle Company finally folded in 1915, it was the plethora of homesteaders who had settled along the Huerfano, Apishapa, and Purgatoire Rivers that helped drive the company out of business. These smaller settlers fenced off their property with strands of barbwire; they also took their problems to the courts and initiated a blizzard of lawsuits that proved a major drain on the financial resources of the big barons. The era of open-range ranching stuttered to a close. A few lesser outfits such as Rourke Ranch, located deep

Rourke Ranch, Picketwire
Canyon.

inside Picketwire Canyon, managed to hold on. Founded by Eugene Rourke
in 1869, the ranch remained in the hands of the same family for three
generations, expanding from its original homestead allotment to an impressive 73,500 acres.

I was confident that I'd be able to hoof it all the way to Rourke Ranch,
8.7 miles from my point of entry, but after about an hour I wasn't too sure.
It was hot down in the canyon. I'd brought two big jugs of water, balanced
on each hip like a pair of clumsy Colt .44s. Bing, you're dead, I muttered,
drawing my finger up from my right hip and fanning an imaginary hammer
at a playful magpie pecking gravel in the dirt path ahead of me. Already I
was beginning to hallucinate, and I hadn't been inside the canyon for more
than an hour. The heat trapped between the distant walls seemed to swell
like bread dough. Up top there no doubt was a wind, hot and chapping,
skirling like a sirocco over the grass. Down here a faint breeze fluttered
through the cottonwoods.

There was little shade, and at each tree, basking in whatever shadow it
cast, I swallowed a mouthful of tepid water and wiped my glistening face
with a bandanna. A faint hissing tickled my ears, which I took for a testy
rattler but which turned out to be the sound of the Purgatoire running over
a scree of loose stones. The river at this point inched diagonally across the

Rourke Ranch stable showing Spanish construction.

grassy bottoms, angling from wall to wall. Despite the heat, the suffocating closeness, I liked it down here. The topside world seemed a long way off, connected to this close, stifling place by a tenuous cord. Around each new bend I kept thinking I'd come across a lost *placita* full of people wearing sombreros, carded wool garments, leather boots with jingling rowels, loading up a caravan of pack mules. Nearly 4 miles into the hike I did pass the ruins of the Dolores Mission and Cemetery, built between 1871 and 1889, when Hispanic pioneers first began settling in the canyon. I paused at a little graveyard of weathered headstones, enclosed by a rusty wire fence, and took another swig of water and tried to imagine what the Dolores Mission must have looked like in full swing a hundred or more years ago: cattle bawling, people calling, roosters crowing, sheep and goats braying; lives unfolding in the depths of this distant place, so far away from everywhere else.

A hooded oriole flashed between two shrubs. An eastern bird, succored by the flora growing in the canyon, nesting this far west along the sheltered corridor of the river valley. A hundred and fifty years ago, there would have been elk inside this drainage, antelope and grizzly bear. I wouldn't dare traipse through these depths without a pistol, a Bowie knife, and a Hawken .54-caliber rifle. At one point, maybe a hundred yards ahead, on a long treeless stretch of trail, I saw the outline of a huge longhorn. The original steer, the prototype of the meat-bearing bovid that provided the genetic foundation for the subsequent infestation of Great Plains cattle. I looked around for a tree to climb—longhorns are not to be messed with—but there were no trees at this juncture. Fortunately, the outline turned out to be a dark rock shellacked with desert varnish that had calved off from the top of the cliff and tumbled down to the edge of the trail.

Here in Picketwire, as well as other canyons in southeast Colorado, Native people down through the millennia have pecked out mysterious whorls and squiggles in the dark, glistening patina of the rocks. According to modern dating techniques, some of these sites go back nearly 5,000 years. We don't have enough information to determine who these prehistoric occupants were, where they came from, why they stayed, how they utilized the biological resources, or what compelled them to leave. Four hundred years ago, at the time of first contact between Europeans and Natives, Apache or Apachean-related groups most likely dwelt in the canyon or had access to its resources. Subsequent to them, Kiowa, Comanche, Arapaho, and Cheyenne people occupied parts of the area. The exact meaning of the figures and abstract lines chipped out of the brittle overlay of oxidized moisture mantling many of the rocks isn't known. Maybe someday we will be able to decipher their arcane code.

At slightly over 5 miles, after a forced march that left me wondering about the future of my toes, I reached the site of the dinosaur footprints, the largest aggregation of petrified tracks in North America. The site extends about a quarter of a mile, mostly along the east bank of the Purgatoire River. Someone who bothered to count claims there are over

Gravestone, Dolores Mission, Picketwire Canyon.

Brontosaurus tracks, Picketwire Canyon.

1,300 individual prints, left around 150 million years ago by two domi-
nant types of antediluvian creatures, allosaurs and brontosaurs.

The sun popped and fizzled like a burning flare. The ranger on duty at
the Comanche Grasslands Visitor Center had warned me not to walk in
Picketwire Canyon by myself. "If you turn your ankle or pass out from
dehydration, we won't find you for a few days," she said. "The coyotes and
buzzards will already have made a mess of your parts." She was a pretty
woman with blue eyes and wispy blond hair. "People misjudge the place.
They don't realize how difficult it can be. It can swallow an outsider like a
snake. I make my husband take a gun when we go in there."

I paused to munch a sandwich at the side of the river in the flimsy
shade of a mesquite tree. The majority of the petrified tracks were visible
on the other bank, intagliated in a field of what looked like chalky white
mud. The river was running high, fed by snowmelt dribbling off the Spanish Peaks, a frothy, lactescent current that hissed and slathered in time with
my hungry chewing. I could have crossed to the other side to inspect the
tracks more closely, but I elected not to. I'd have had to take off my boots
and wade the river, and I didn't know what would happen to my feet if I
did. My toes felt achy and swollen; once I removed the boots, I didn't know
whether I could squeeze them back on. I was afraid my feet might ooze out
in a bubbling torrent of liquid flesh. A gluey eruption that would stick to
the rocks like a pair of spongy pedestals and force me to remain upright in
place while the sun baked my brain to a gritty cinder. I drank as much
water as I could, but it tasted gummy and foul. The tracks on the opposite
bank glimmered like a bed of salt. I tried to envision a band of Jurassic
reptiles plodding along the edge of a dank, humid lake edged with ferns and
rubbery plants, the surface of the water churning with the movements of
ferocious ichthyosaurs gliding below.

A panoply of vivid images—dinosaurs, bison, Indians, longhorns, cow-
boys—swirled before my eyes, mixing, mingling, garbling their outlines in
a messy stew of hybrid figures. The tortured shades of Bonilla and Humana,
conquistadors who perished in these depths in the 1590s without final
absolution—hence the name "Purgatory"—danced through my torrid brain.

It's time to go, I decided, and clambered to my feet and began limping
back the way I'd come, in the opposite direction of Rourke Ranch, which
I would have to leave for another time.

The Treasure Wagon

Reportedly, there's a wagon down in Picketwire Canyon, drawn by six black horses and driven by a masked driver who wears a pair of luminous gloves. The wagon darts from shadow to shadow, so fast that nobody has ever really seen it. Over the years the legend has grown that the driver is a Spaniard carrying a stack of treasure to a special hiding place that has never been discovered. And who the strange man urging the dark horses on has never been determined.

18
King Coal

Coal was one of the most important resources to the expanding U.S. economy in the first part of the twentieth century. Colorado, along with Pennsylvania and West Virginia, was a major mining state in the nation. The Spanish Peaks region contained rich deposits of bituminous ("soft") coal, much of it glimmering in visible seams along the surface of the semi-arid ridges and hills of the lower slopes of the twin summits.

Following the Civil War, coal became the primary fuel for the American industrial machine. West of the Mississippi, significant deposits of soft coal were discovered in Colorado and Wyoming. The first mines in the Spanish Peaks were dug in the 1860s. The arrival of the railroad in the mid-1870s accelerated the volume and pace. The first wave of miners—mainly single men, itinerants, with little interest in settling down—hailed from Britain, Ireland, and northern Europe. The same trains that brought them to the Spanish Peaks transported tons of black ore to the mills in Pueblo. By the late 1880s, coal had supplanted ranching as the region's primary industry; in 1887 the Sopris Mine, a few miles east of Trinidad, began to boom. In the wake of Sopris, companies opened new mines farther up the Purgatoire Valley and around Walsenburg and La Veta.

The next wave of miners, mostly family men, came mainly from central and eastern Europe. The majority were impoverished with no political clout, few spoke English, as many as one-third were illiterate. They belonged to different ethnic groups, with little in common, and tended to remain locked within their linguistic enclaves.

Coal mining in Colorado in the early 1900s was a hazardous business. Between 1910 and 1913, 618 miners lost their lives in mine-related accidents.

Coal-mining mural, La Veta.

Colorado's dry climate generated high levels of suspended dust, which increased the possibility of explosions. Severe geologic upheavals had weakened the rock around the coal seams, making cave-ins more frequent than in eastern or midwestern mines. Simple safety procedures were largely ignored. When asked why his mine shafts weren't properly shored up with timber posts, a Colorado Fuel & Iron (CF&I) official said, "Dagoes are cheaper than props" (quoted in Papanikolas, p. 38).

This attitude prevailed at the top and trickled down through every management layer of the southern Colorado coal companies. The major owners were largely indifferent to the workers' plight. John D. Rockefeller Jr., majority stockholder of CF&I, a company that owned several Spanish Peaks coalfields, was born into a stifling volume of wealth, which prevented him from understanding the workers' problems. Consistently, throughout the region's worst labor disputes, he refused to acknowledge the right of workers to belong to a union. "All serious troubles have been caused by labor organizations trying to force their regime on the businesses against the wishes of the workingmen and their employers," he declared (quoted in Vallejo, p. 90).

In 1892 and again in 1903, southern Colorado miners went out on strike. They demanded an eight-hour day, semimonthly pay, the abolition

of company scrip, independent weighmen instead of those employed by the companies, and a better supply of pure air down in the shafts as mandated by state law. (Many beneficial laws existed on the books, which the companies ignored and state and federal agencies chose not to enforce.)

The 1903 strike lasted four months. Company spies infiltrated the ranks of the strikers. Private police were hired to harass them. The real crunch came when the Colorado state militia rounded up between four and five hundred strikers, herded them onto trains bound for Kansas and New Mexico, and kicked them off in the middle of nowhere with dire warnings never to return.

For ten long years the miners nursed their grievances. Better organization was the key to success, and several years prior to the 1913 walkout the United Mine Workers (UMW) union sent veteran organizer John R. Lawson to the Spanish Peaks as part of a concerted effort to organize all the coal miners in the state. Lawson was indefatigable in his efforts, and by summer of 1913 he had enrolled an impressive number of miners as UMW members.

In September 1913 at a convention in Trinidad, the miners voted to walk out on the twenty-third of the month unless the owners met their demands. Despite the sacrifices in 1903, most miners still worked twelve hours a day instead of eight. Pay ranged from 29 cents an hour to a maximum of $3.50 a day. (In 1911 the most productive coal miner in Colorado earned around $696 the entire year.) Wages were calibrated according to how much coal a miner could extract in a single day. Company weighmen,

Coal cart, Walsenburg.

Building facades, downtown
Trinidad.

operating the scales, subtracted everything they could; to earn credit for
digging a ton of coal, a miner usually had to submit around 2,400 pounds.

Many miners were still paid in company scrip, which they used to buy
groceries and pay their rent. Prices were usually higher in company stores
than in Trinidad or Walsenburg. Company bars in the mining camps served
company whiskey and beer. If a miner needed a loan, the company was
happy to offer him one at a higher rate of interest than what he would pay
at a local bank.

The miners' demands were basically the same as what they had opted
for ten years earlier: an eight-hour workday, the right to choose any doctor
or boarding place they wished, pay for "dead work" (timbering, cleaning,
picking slate, and the like), and, of course, recognition of the UMW as
their bargaining agent.

The owners dug in their heels. They refused to acknowledge the union
or to discuss any other critical issues. Colorado Governor Elias Ammons
sent representatives to dissuade the miners from walking out. The U.S.
Department of Labor sent officials to Colorado to confer with both parties.
The Labor Department tried to reach Rockefeller in New York but failed
to persuade him to intercede. "We would rather the unfortunate conditions
should continue and that we should lose all the millions invested," Rockefeller

said, "than that American workingmen should be deprived of their right, under the Constitution, to work for whom they please" (quoted in Vallejo, p. 90). President Woodrow Wilson wrote letters to the owners asking them to meet with the union and avert a crisis, but his request was ignored.

On September 23, 1913, in a blinding snowstorm, several thousand miners and their families moved out or were evicted from the company towns in the Trinidad and Walsenburg areas. Tent colonies were set up in a half-dozen sites, the biggest at Ludlow, 12 miles northwest of Trinidad, where about nine hundred miners settled down in about 180 tents provided by the UMW. Many of these communities were strategically placed at the mouths of canyons so nonstriking miners had to pass through them to get to work.

Soon after the strike began, Governor Ammons called out several units of the state militia, which set up base camps at Trinidad and Walsenburg. Within a few weeks soldiers were patrolling the entire Spanish Peaks area. Smaller camps were established near trouble spots to monitor their activities.

Tension between the two sides mounted with each passing week. Sporadic gunfire was exchanged. Periodically, the miners touched off a dynamite charge. Dead bodies began showing up along the railroad. To protect their women and children, the strikers dug deep pits under the tents, not only at Ludlow but at the other camps as well.

As the months dragged on, the state militia's period of service expired, and the soldiers were replaced by professional strikebreakers, many from the Baldwin-Felts Detective Agency in Denver, which had provided a similar service during the 1903 strike. These guards, or "goons," as they were frequently called, obtained their authorization by being sworn in as deputy sheriffs in both Huerfano and Las Animas Counties. In response, union organizers were sworn in as game wardens so they could legally carry guns.

Six weeks before the strike, on August 6, Gerald Lippiat, a union organizer, pulled a gun on two Baldwin-Felts operatives in Trinidad and was shot dead; one of the operatives was out on bail for a murder charge in West Virginia. On October 24, 1913, striking miners protested the attempt of the wife of a scab worker to join her husband at the Walsen Mine, even though the miners had threatened to blow up her house if she didn't vacate the premises. A crowd gathered in front of the house; guards sent by the company to protect the woman and her children were fired on. The guards retaliated, killing three strikers.

Baldwin-Felts agents hustled up by train from Trinidad with a machine gun, which they set up on the steps of the Huerfano County Courthouse in the center of Walsenburg. Four days later Governor Ammons signed an executive order mobilizing the rest of the national guard. During the first few weeks the soldiers did their job, disarming strikers and police with equal impartiality, but as their period of enlistment expired, they were replaced by strikebreakers with minimal sympathy for the miners' cause. The violence escalated on both sides; in October, state militia raked the Forbes tent colony with gunfire, killing one man and wounding a young

Staircase to YMCA, Oakview Mine, near La Veta.

boy. On November 8, 1913, strikers ambushed five mine workers in their vehicle on a lonely road west of La Veta, killing four.

In the meantime, a consortium of Denver bankers loaned the state of Colorado the necessary funds to maintain the militia and pay off the scabs who had been imported from Texas, Kansas, and New Mexico to work in the mines. (By January 1914, CF&I alone had brought in 1,400 scabs to take the place of the striking miners.) While Governor Ammons stopped short of officially placing the Spanish Peaks area under martial law, he did place the strike zone under the control of militia commander Gen. John Chase, a pompous man with military pretensions who helped break the Cripple Creek strike in 1903–1904. Complicating any real understanding of the problem was the fact that the absentee owners of the CF&I accepted unquestioningly the assessment of the local situation made by their representatives in southern Colorado and thus declined to intervene in an area they regarded as the responsibility of local management.

The months passed. The year 1913 rolled into 1914. More armed strikers began digging trenches along the railroad embankments and in the arroyos outside the tent cities. As March turned into April, the violence escalated. Strikers shot out the searchlights the militia trained on the tent cities; in response, the militia filled the night air with rifle and machine-gun fire.

On January 4, 1914, Mother Jones—eighty-three years old, legendary champion of workers' rights—was arrested in Trinidad. She was put back onboard the train that had brought her down from Denver and returned to the capital. A week later she was back in Trinidad, where she was arrested again and placed in Mount San Rafael Hospital without writ of habeas corpus. On January 22 her unlawful detention precipitated a march by over a thousand women carrying banners and flags. They were met in force by mounted troops under the command of General Chase who drew their sabers and charged, injuring six women and scoring a huge moral victory for the protestors. During the fracas a woman jabbed her hat pin into the flank of General Chase's horse, which reared up, throwing him to the ground.

The U.S. House of Representatives finally authorized its Committee on Mines and Mining to investigate the Colorado coal strike. Hearings in Denver convened on February 9, 1914. The publicity proved beneficial to the miners; by the end of the month, General Chase withdrew nearly a thousand troops from the strike zone, which helped ease tensions. On April 17 Governor Ammons pulled the remaining troops from the Spanish Peaks region, except for two companies composed of the worst thugs and hooligans.

The archvillain of this tragic story was Lt. Karl E. Linderfelt of the Colorado State Militia, a self-styled martinet and bullyboy whose blatant cruelty made his own men uneasy. Linderfelt had served with the U.S. Army in the Philippines (1899–1900), where he participated in a vicious counterinsurgency war fueled by racial hatred. His temper was volatile; he despised the strikers' lowly origins with a fierce, xenophobic contempt. Dressed in a crisp uniform, complete with tie and flat-brimmed campaign hat, he looked down from his tall horse upon the grimy miners with utter disdain. "I am Jesus Christ, and my men on horses are Jesus Christs, and we must be obeyed!" he screamed at them (quoted in Beshoar, p. 124).

With the removal of the troops, what should have been an improved situation turned worse. On the morning of April 20, 1914, the air around the Ludlow tent colony was rocked by dynamite blasts. The militia under Linderfelt's command, which had taken a position on a hill overlooking the camp, responded with rifle and machine-gun fire. The strikers fired back, and a prolonged battle commenced that sent many women and children fleeing out of Ludlow into the shelter of the nearby arroyos. The shooting lasted well into the afternoon when the strikers began to run out of ammunition. Militiamen then attacked, igniting the tents with flaming brooms dipped in coal oil; when the smoke cleared, the suffocated bodies of two women and nine children were found in a bunker under one of the tents.

Over the years the number of victims of the Ludlow Massacre has been greatly exaggerated. The best possible estimate by reliable historians stands at two women, eleven children, six or seven strikebreakers, and one militia guard. Louis Tikas, charismatic leader of the Greek miners, was detained by the militia and brought before Karl Linderfelt, who smashed a

United Mine Workers monument to Ludlow Massacre victims.

rifle butt against his head, severely gashing his skull. Three steel-jacketed
bullets, ostensibly fired from militia rifles, were later found in his back to
make it look like he'd been shot while trying to escape. Tikas was enormously popular and respected throughout the Ludlow community. A few
days after his death, a mass funeral was held in Trinidad that was attended
by sympathizers from all over the state, including John Lawson and Mother
Jones. A double row of mourners stretching more than a mile filed up
Main and into Commercial Street behind the black funeral coach, followed
by five hundred Greek miners and two thousand men and women, their
feet treading a solemn tattoo against the brick-cobbled streets.

What followed the Ludlow debacle has become known as the Ten Days
War, or the Great Coalfield War. It raged on both sides of the Spanish
Peaks, with scores of people killed. Said historian M. Edmund Vallejo,
"During this time, incidents occurred between the striking miners and
their adversaries that probably have not been equaled for their viciousness
in any industrial conflict in American history" (Vallejo, p. 96). Anarchy and
open rebellion prevailed. Private vendettas were carried out under the broad
umbrella of social protest. Armed miners swarmed into Trinidad with revo-
lutionary fervor. Brandishing rifles, they tramped the streets wearing red
bandannas and singing their favorite song:

> Union forever, hurrah boys hurrah!
> Up with the union and down with the law,
> For we're coming, Colorado, we're coming all the way,
> Shouting the battle cry of freedom.

The mayor and sheriff fled. The townspeople cowered in their homes,
but the strikers policed the streets day and night, and no one was hurt.
Outside the town, however, along the narrow canyons, the strikers torched
every coal company facility they could find in Huerfano and Las Animas
Counties. Governor Ammons finally had to ask President Woodrow Wilson to send in federal troops.

On April 27, a week after the Ludlow battle, new fighting erupted in
Walsenburg. Three hundred armed strikers deployed along the hogback
north of town and besieged the CF&I-owned Walsen and McNally Mines.
The mine guards retaliated; bullets whined and ricocheted through the
streets, killing more than a dozen people and wounding many more. Three
days later federal troops debarked from a train, and the strikers withdrew.
The Ten Days War was over. An uneasy peace settled over the region,
though the strike dragged on until December 7, 1914.

News of the Ludlow Massacre sent shock waves through the nation.
"This battle was from the first a deliberate effort of the soldiers to assault
the tent-colony, with purpose to burn, pillage and kill," Max Eastman,
editor of the socialist magazine *The Masses,* fulminated (Eastman, p. 157).
Four hundred indictments were eventually brought against the strikers;
UMW organizer John Lawson was convicted of murder charges, but that
verdict was later set aside by the Colorado Supreme Court.

The unionization of the mines was dealt a serious blow by the introduction of the Rockefeller Plan, brokered by W. L. Mackenzie King, former Canadian labor minister, later prime minister of Canada. The plan proved the prototype of the paternalistic "company union" concept where workers could recommend changes while the company retained full control over the decisionmaking process.

In September 1915, in a belated gesture of reconciliation, John D. Rockefeller Jr. visited Colorado amid much fanfare; his arrival was touted by the local conservative press as nothing short of the Second Coming. Rockefeller in many ways was a fine, upstanding man; certainly he used his enormous personal fortune to contribute to many worthwhile causes and charities. Unlike his tall, dour, pinched-face father, John Jr. was stocky and plump, with a smooth, fleshy face and pleasant manner. He was deeply religious, often lecturing to his Sunday School classes about the virtues of capitalism. In Colorado he did his best to behave like a regular fellow; he ate and danced with the miners and their wives and bounced their children on his knee. Mackenzie King accompanied him, and as the two magnates journeyed from camp to camp, they tried as best they could to mollify the raw feelings left in the wake of the brutal strike.

"We are partners," Rockefeller declared with a hearty smile, but his efforts to substitute philanthropy for justice were not warmly received. He lacked the imaginative resources to properly understand the real problems the miners faced. He ordered new bandstands and pavilions for many of the coal camps, new meeting houses, shower stalls, and baseball fields, but the issues for which the people fought and died remained basically unchanged.

The massacre focused nationwide attention on the conditions in the mines. Sympathy for the United Mine Workers increased enormously. In 1915 the Colorado Industrial Commission was formed to mediate differences between labor and management. The first-ever Colorado Workman's Compensation Act was established. But it wasn't until the Wagner Act was passed in 1938 during Franklin Roosevelt's New Deal that the company union was outlawed and the United Mine Workers was officially recognized as the negotiating agent for miners throughout the nation.

The Golden Mummy

Two men at Coyote Mine on Silver Mountain one winter day in 1892 had just finished working when snow started to fall. To avoid being marooned by a blizzard, they took a shortcut over the mountain. While crossing a steep slope the ground gave way, and they fell into a cave about 8 feet wide and 30 or 40 feet deep. Near the opening, one of the men touched the form of a child resting on a niche. When they tried to lift the form, they found it hard and extremely heavy. In the feeble light of a mining candle, they discerned that the figure was made of solid gold. But the snow was beginning to pile up outside, and they knew if they didn't get moving they would be trapped inside the cave. The following spring, when they returned, all traces of the hole they had fallen through had disappeared.

19
The Feast of St. Ignatius

The church stands a half-block off Colorado 12 near the center of the little town of Segundo. It's a pretty church with a tall belfry peaked by an imposing cross. The outside walls are painted white with green trim. The gutters edging the tin roof are also painted green, which accentuates the church's tidy profile.

Albert Mattie waves to us as we enter through the front door and settle in a pew on the right side of the aisle. Albert's a nervous little man in a blue banlon shirt and blue polyester pants with slash pockets. He confers with members of the modest choir, presumably about the hymns they will sing later that morning. The choir sits in a paneled alcove near the altar. A santo of St. Ignatius perches in a recessed niche at the back of the alcove. Next to it stands the organ, with the organist balanced on a rickety stool, leafing through a sheet of music.

The church feels smaller on the inside than it looks from out in the parking lot. The center aisle leading from the entrance to the altar is insulated with a long strip of beige carpet. Pictures along the side walls depict the Stations of the Cross. A banner draped across the pulpit reads "Peace to All Who Enter." The altar is bedecked with flowers and small carvings. It's Sunday, July 25, the Feast of St. Ignatius, and the congregation is slowly assembling to celebrate the life of the founder of the Jesuit Order.

People trickle in, mainly older men and women with pale Hispanic faces. They nod to one another, shake hands, take each other by the wrist, smile, and mumble greetings. The atmosphere is subdued and reverent. Several young families enter—women clad in plain dresses, men in creased pants and pressed white shirts, children in Sunday finery with their hair

St. Ignatius Church, Segundo.

coiffed or, in the case of the boys, slicked back along the contours of their skulls. Five minutes before the service begins, people slip through the front and side doors but with no evident haste, in a leisurely manner born of habit and practice, the product of generations of worship by the same families at the same church. A few minutes later the organist squares herself around on the stool and settles her feet on the pedals and presses her fingers against the keys; a deep, throaty hum reverberates from the pipes, which silences the idle chatter drifting through the air and signals the congregation that the service is about to begin. The priest, an elderly, white-haired man decked out in a bright green surplice, steps to the pulpit and in a high-pitched raspy voice welcomes the congregation to a morning of worship in honor of the memory and accomplishments of St. Ignatius of Loyola, after whom the church is named.

As a non-Catholic, my knowledge of St. Ignatius is sketchy. Before the service commences, Albert Mattie, thoughtful as always, slips a pamphlet between my fingers with some details of the saint's life. Ignatius was born in Spain in 1491. He joined the army as a young man and was severely wounded during the siege of Pamplona. Upon recovering, he turned to the church for solace and inspiration. During a retreat at the famous monastery of Montserrat, he wrote *The Book of Spiritual Exercises*. His avowed aim for the rest of his life was simple: to work for the greater glory of God under the direction of the papal father. In 1537 he founded the Society of Jesus (Jesuits), which was bound by laws of poverty, chastity, and hard work on behalf of others. Ignatius died in 1556 and was canonized in 1622.

Midway through the service, led by the padre with the altar boy bearing the cross—with Albert and another man carrying silk banners trimmed with fluttering tassels—the entire congregation filed outside and circled the church in a slow, stately procession, singing a hymn in Spanish. The sky was clear, the air scintillant. The town of Segundo is located in the valley of the Purgatoire River on the south slopes of the Spanish Peaks, 20 miles west of Trinidad. There must have been fifty or sixty people in the procession. Old, young, in-between, walking in double rows, singing in ragged voices over the warble of pigeons clustered on the telephone wires.

The Feast of San Isidro is another important day in the lives of the people of the Spanish Peaks. San Isidro is celebrated in the spring, shortly after Easter, usually in mid-May just before planting time. In the old days, in villages like Segundo the feast began the night before when people gathered at the community chapel to place an image of San Isidro on a platform festooned with plants and boughs. To the rhythm of chanted prayers and melodious hymns, the villagers filed out of the church in a long procession, down onto the bottomlands, across the Purgatoire River, and up to the high ground on the other side. The image was then taken from the platform and placed within a green bower. An all-night vigil followed, punctuated by more chants and prayers, illuminated by strings of winking candles. A pair of singers (*rezadores*) sang the stanzas of the hymns, while the people intoned the chorus. This devotional offering was interrupted by a communal

San Ysidro procession. Patron
saint of fields.

meal served at midnight. The first rays of morning light that illuminated the
face of San Isidro signaled the end of the festivity. The saint was removed
from the bower and placed back on the platform. It was then borne at the
head of the procession, back through the fields in the valley all the way to
the plaza, where it was returned to its place in the chapel.

After the service we filed into an annex across the parking lot from the
church for a supper, which the women of the church had prepared. The
food was set up on long tables banquet-style. We heaped our plates with
sliced turkey and dressing, green beans, mashed potatoes and gravy, tossed
salad, jello cubes swirled with whipped cream. We chatted with the priest,
a genial man of French extraction from St. Louis, who told us that his date
of birth was October 24, 1929, "Black Thursday," the day the stock market
crashed. "Not such a promising occasion," he said with a grin, "but I guess
it turned out okay. It was tough being a kid in the Depression. The whole
family had to pull together. I delivered newspapers and worked in a drug-
store. My dad was a garbage collector, which was quite a comedown from
his previous employment as an insurance agent. It all seems like a bad
dream now. Or maybe a good one. I think maybe life was more real back
then. I hesitate to equate hardship and reality, but it's the hard times we

Penitente reading from *cuaderno* during Feast of San Ysidro.

Bob Tapia, Cokedale.

remember best, when we're put to the test, and not so much when things are soft."

I was scraping my fork through a splot of congealed gravy at the center of my plate when a thin, bony fellow with a droopy face sat down across from me. A ball cap covered what appeared to be a hairless skull. The coppery tint of his face was slatted with wrinkles and folds. His dark eyes were moist and deeply slotted. He ate slowly from his plate, chewing each bite in a methodical manner before gulping it down. He nodded cordially, and I nodded back. I sipped my glass of lemonade, giving him time to consume the turkey and potatoes on his plate. The padre had suggested I try and speak with this fellow, whose name was Bob Tapia. For practically all his professional life he'd been a miner, working the pits all over the Spanish Peaks. "He might have something to say," the padre whispered before picking up his plate and departing. "I'll send him over. He likes to talk."

Indeed he did. Some people like to talk but don't say much. Others like Bob Tapia seem to have an instinctive sense of what it takes to tell a story. When he had finished eating, he pushed the plate away with his long, knotty fingers and sat back in the hard metal chair. "Father Gene tells me you're writing some kind of book."

"That's right. About the Spanish Peaks. He tells me you were a coal miner."

"Uh-huh. I begun when I was fourteen, and I stopped fifty years later when I was sixty-four."

"How old are you now?"

"I was born in nineteen hundert and nine. So that makes me . . . "

"Nearly ninety."

A smile cracked his dark, leathery face, splitting his baggy cheeks from ear to ear. "You must be a college boy, the way you add and subtract." His teeth were white and prominent.

"Father Gene tells me you were at Ludlow when the massacre took place."

"Well, not exactly. I wasn't there during the fighting. I was there a few days before, staying with relatives in the tents. Two days before the shooting started, my dad come and got me and took me back to our house in Goldnar, up in Berwind Canyon, which wasn't too far away. No, I missed the actual fight, which I can't say I'm sorry about. Lots of people got killed that day."

He recrossed his legs and placed his right hand, spotty with what appeared to be little granules of dark, gritty dust, on the handle of his cane. "See, I come from miners. All my people was miners. Grandfather, uncle, father. They all worked in the mines practically till the day they died. My uncle lost a leg in the mines."

"What did you do in the mines?"

"I did just about everything a man can do, except I never was a foreman. I didn't have the education for that. I drove mules. I was a timberman. I weighed coal when they brought it out. I was a driller. Top job I had was tipple boss. Best job I had was weighman. I liked working with the scales and counting up the pounds those fellows brought out. The best could excavate more than a ton in a single day. Down on their knees, swinging a pick at the seam. That's how they was paid, according to the amount they busted loose and carried out on the trains."

"What do you remember about Ludlow?"

"I heard gunshots all day. I remember that. Bang-bang-bang. Sometimes rat-tat-tat from the machine guns the militia had on their side. Now and then a deep thump from a bomb or dynamite going off. It was a hell of a battle. I remember my dad taking me to Trinidad for Louis Tikas's funeral. All these miners walking the streets in a long line, not saying a word. The sound their feet made against the stones—knock-knock-knock."

Bob rapped the knuckles of his right hand against the table top.

"Mother Jones was there, too. I remember seeing her, this little old lady dressed in black, at the head of the line. She made a speech, too. She could talk a blue streak and cuss like a miner."

"Tapia. Your last name. Is that Italian?"

"Spanish. My paternal grandfather was named Cabeza de Vaca. He was the only survivor of an Indian attack. Everybody was killed and all the wagons set on fire. He was left for dead but was still breathing when the rescuers showed up. A Spanish family named Tapia took him in and adopted him."

"Wow."

"He was a real *viejo.* I mean, he had a face that could stop you in your tracks. People don't look that way anymore."

"What do we look like now?"

"We all look like each other," Bob said, flashing his shiny teeth. "We all look like we've been carved out of the same bar of soap."

He chuckled at his own observation. "I got black lung from working in the mines. Everyone who worked got black lung. You inhale that coal dust all day, there's no way you can avoid it."

"But doesn't it usually kill people off early?"

"Well, I was diagnosed in my fifties. So I stopped smoking. I still got it. I still wheeze and spit up little bits of charcoal. But I ain't dead yet. And I really don't know why."

"So all the mines are closed now?"

"Last mine, the Allen mine, closed about ten years ago. I worked in every one of them mines, up and down this valley."

"Purgatoire?"

"Here and up in Berwind Canyon. See, in my younger days I could get a job at any mine I wanted."

"Why's that?"

"'Cause I could play baseball."

"Yeah? What position did you play?"

"I played lots of positions. But the position I played best was catcher. I could hit okay, nothing great. But I could field, and I had a strong arm, and

I could throw out runners trying to steal. I threw hard and I threw straight. Coaches like that. Catcher's the most important position on the team. You got a good catcher, and it's easier to win games."

He twirled a spoon through his coffee cup. "See, each mining camp had its own ball team. They all played each other, and they had some pretty good rivalries. Oh, baseball brought me lots of jobs. I played semipro for a while with a Pueblo team. We'd get twenty-five dollars a game. This was during the Depression, and that was a lot of money. In 1936 I had a chance to try out with the Brooklyn Dodgers. They sent a scout to Pueblo, and I was down here and didn't have enough money for gas, so I didn't try out. Who knows, maybe I'd of made it to the majors. But I didn't have enough money to buy me a few gallons of gas so I could drive up there."

"How do you feel about that?"

He shrugged. "There's not any way I can feel. That's just what happened, and you can't do nothing about it."

He rapped his knuckles against the table again and looked away for a moment. "I played with Billy Martin one time."

"Of the Yankees?"

"That's right. He come down from Fort Carson just to see me play. This was during the war. 'You should be in the majors,' he said. 'You're that good.' But then a foul tip injured my knee, and I wasn't so good after that. That foul tip hurt worse than anything that ever happened to me in the mines."

He looked off again. "But that's okay. I got a lot out of baseball, even if I never made it to the pros."

"So what now?"

"I'm takin' it easy. I live with my son in a house in Cokedale. When the weather gets bad, I go live with my other son in Palm Springs. It's been a good life. When I first retired I did a lot of hunting. I love to hunt, but I can't do it no more. Deer, elk, duck, quail. I love the taste of that wild stuff."

He lapsed into silence. Maybe the meal had made him sleepy. His eyelids fluttered and his head seemed to nod.

"It's been a pleasure talking with you."

"You take care, young fellow, and come back and see us."

"I'd like to speak with you again."

"Any time, young fellow. Any time."

The Legend of San Isidro

A humble, hard-working peasant named Isidro once lived in a fertile valley in Peru. With his two oxen and wooden plow he worked his land from dawn till dusk. The climate in the valley was perfect; a long growing season and plentiful rain contributed to the bountiful crops he produced each year. He always had plenty of food for his family. He took such pride in his accomplishments that he neglected God in his thoughts and feelings.

One day as he plowed his fields, he heard someone calling. Several times he heard the call but continued to plow. The last time the voice sounded loud and clear. It was a messenger from God, who told Isidro that if he didn't pay more homage to God an evil person would be sent as his neighbor. It took a little while, but after Isidro clearly understood the message, he stopped plowing and fell on his knees in the rich black soil and begged God to spare him the curse of an evil neighbor. Thereafter, Isidro always took time to say his prayers, and his land continued to produce abundant crops.

20
The Power of Twice

One day in mid-October I poked along a road that wound back into the peaks. Glowering cliffs blocked the light, gloomy shadows settled between the trees, the road slanted upward at an alarming angle. In low gear, engine rumbling, I slipped through Little Kansas, a settlement of rough-hewn log cabins and A-frames tucked in a dark grove alongside Wahatoya Creek. Little Kansas was founded by flatlanders back in the 1930s, eager to escape dust storms, summer heat, chapping winds, and the dreary monotony of the Great Plains. How they must have relished the relief these cool, bosky folds gave them! A secluded verticality, which made them invisible to everyone but themselves, out of sight of the rest of the world, secretive and anonymous.

Past the settlement the road dwindled to a trail. There were still several hours of daylight left, but this deep into the mountain the trail turned dark and unfriendly. I got back in the car, wheeled around, and bumped back down the track. At the edge of the settlement I encountered a man out for a stroll with his dog. He was from Texas, and he'd spent most of the summer up here in the shade of the trees. It was hotter in San Antonio than it had been in a decade, and he was retired, and he didn't see why he shouldn't spend the entire summer in this soothing place, falling asleep every night to the sound of Wahatoya Creek splashing down East Spanish Peak.

He was suspicious at first, but after I told him why I was there we chatted amicably. "Lots of bears this summer," he remarked. "That's one reason I like it here. We don't have bears in San Antonio, except at the zoo. Here, you can see one every day."

The man's age was indecipherable, somewhere between forty-five and seventy. He obviously had taken good care of himself. He was lean and tan and appeared quite capable of walking the 8 miles back to La Veta if he had to. He wore his hair in a flattop. Wireframe glasses gave his sharp features a thoughtful air. He spoke without trace of an accent, in smooth, manicured tones, like an airline pilot.

"The other day something happened I've not seen before in all the years I've been coming here. A bear got into the house across from mine. He worked the back door loose and crept inside, and when I saw him he was prowling around the kitchen. I could see his head through the window as he rummaged around the drawers and cabinets, looking for something to eat. He looked so much at home you'd swear he was getting ready to put dinner on the table. I stood on the porch of my house, peering at him through binoculars. I thought if he didn't clear out after a while I'd call the Forest Service or the Fish and Wildlife people. I've got a gun, but I didn't want to shoot him. And yet I know the people who own the house, and I didn't want him to trash the premises. We try and look out for each other up here. We're kind of isolated, which is why so many of us come back year after year. Well, as it turned out, I didn't have to do either one. The bear banged around a bit more. At one point he leaned over the sink. I know that kitchen; I've been in the house many times. He looked like a person running water over a dish. Then he straightened up, and the next thing I know he tottered onto the back porch, sniffed the air, and disappeared into the trees. His mouth was powdered white, so he must have found the sugar."

Later that afternoon I climbed a steep trail leading up to the saddle between the peaks. I was after something, and it wasn't until about an hour later, blowing and puffing, that I realized what it was. I was looking for that midway point between high country and low, between the steepness of the mountains and the gentle, easy glide of the plains. That spot where vertical and horizontal intersect to form an axis that includes the four cardinal directions; a fulcrum of sorts, where I could pause in comfortable repose. It wasn't there in Little Kansas. The terrain was too severe, the woods too dark, the settlement too isolated. Wahatoya Trail leading up toward the saddle felt more exposed. Late afternoon sunlight sifted between the trees, mournful autumn sunlight, shot through with a sad, aching glow. I had the trail to myself, and in slow, plodding steps I mounted higher and higher toward the saddle. The silence was soothing. Yellow leaves from shedding aspens fluttered to the ground. Squirrels dashed across the duff and litter. Piñon jays swooped from tree to tree. At one point I felt a pair of eyes on me, but that may have been my own paranoia. "Who's out there? Who's watching?" Maybe it was a bear checking me out. "Hello, bear. I mean no harm. I'm looking to dance on the head of a pin between mountains and plains."

The steepness of the climb slowed my pace, and two hours into it I realized I was still a long way from the saddle. The light was failing, and I didn't want to be up there in the dark with no food or overnight equipment, so I tore back down the trail, sliding and skating on the loose pebbles and sticks with all the finesse of a trash can rolling down an alley.

"Double mountains aren't that common in the world. At least those rising from a shared foundation. Spanish Peaks . . . Janus-faced . . . not so much contrasting as complementing the identity of the other. Filling out and augmenting. What if one should take a notion to sail off into space, would the other follow? And what would it look like if it were left alone? We can't conceive of one without the other. Their identities depend upon the presence of the other. In contrast to east peak, west peak looks bigger. In contrast to west peak, east peak is more delicately molded. East peak generates the most legends. West peak attracts more hikers. Their twiceness engenders a cosmos. Together they encompass a world. Singly they replicate little more than their own singularity. In tandem they conflate a universe."

I made these notes in the car after crashing down the Wahatoya Trail, slipping and falling, sprawling on my side, scraping the heel of my right hand. Gravity propelling me in a pathetic simulacrum of flight. Subverting the point of equipoise I had climbed so far to attain.

That night, reading the writings of Zen Master Dōgen, I came upon this passage:

> There are mountains hidden in treasures. There are mountains hidden in swamps. There are mountains hidden in the sky. There are mountains hidden in mountains. There are mountains hidden in hiddenness. This is complete understanding.

"The west peak is masculine, the east feminine," said Gail Ritter who, from the vantage point of the picture window in the front room of her ranch house, has enjoyed a clear and unobstructed view of the mountains for many years. "They are the yin and the yang, the spoken and the unspoken. They embody the concept of the Double, which, more than any other paradigm, best explains who we are and why it's so hard for us to find real contentment in our lives."

I pondered her words as I guided the car out of the mountains that afternoon and down into the Cuchara Valley. Lines of glowing dikes, touched by the setting sun, lay lightly upon the slopes like strands of colorful string. "Everything we do, good or bad," said Gail, "is mirrored by its opposite."

I couldn't quarrel with that. How can you live in close proximity with these features and not contemplate their meaning? Spanish Peaks, so geologically unique, congeal like a mirage on the rim of the horizon. Their duality symbolizes the role the West has played (and continues to play) in the American psyche. New chances, new beginnings, the promise of regeneration. I thought of John Ritter, Gail's grandfather, and the new life he built for himself out West after his terrible ordeal during the Civil War. I thought of the seasonal changes that governed the lives of the Ute

Watermelons, Arkansas River Valley.

Indians. Winter in the lower parks and valleys, summers in the high-lands gathering plants and herbs, spring and fall out on the plains hunting buffalo. (Historian George E. Hyde argues that the Ute were on their way to becoming a bona fide Plains Indian culture when they were stopped by the ferocity of the Comanche, who drove them back to the safety of the mountains.)

We are all transients on this continent, lured by the mythic line of the frontier—that discernible boundary between civilization and wilderness—farther and farther "west." No matter that the line officially vanished (says Frederick Jackson Turner) in the 1890s. It still lingers in our consciousness, and those of us drawn to this country continue to look for it in a thousand different places—around every bend, over every hill, along every river—that place where the land seems commensurate with the yearning for inclusion in our hearts. Once upon a time, bison roamed these grassy slopes, and then they disappeared, and now, as if by subliminal fiat, they are returning, slowly but steadily, on ranches down in the flats. Elk once roamed the grassy plains, but then they were driven up to the heights where they persist to this day, though people who live along the Arkansas River Valley tell me that in the autumn they see them along the bottomlands, heading east out to where they once used to roam. The country not only renews itself for jejune Anglos looking for a meaningful context for their lives but for migrant workers from Mexico in search of a decent wage who pick the fruits and vegetables that grow along the Arkansas River within eyeshot of the twin peaks.

Another alternative the peaks pose (for some folks, at least) revolves around the otherworldly. Of late, UFOs have been sighted on the peaks, though maybe they've always been around. Back then we called them something else—comets, fireballs, shooting stars—whereas today we regard them as harbingers of a future that portends far more than they can ever reveal. Scratch a person who's lived awhile around the peaks and you'll uncover stories of strange sightings and curious phenomena: clouds lingering on certain cliffs; lightning striking the same location; wreaths of Saint Elmo's fire curling across the rocks; puzzling air currents that flow when they should ebb; places at the foot of certain buttes infested with rattlesnakes, which some people regard as portals to parallel universes. "There's definitely something here," said a longtime resident who prefers to remain unnamed. "I've seen things I'd rather not talk about. There's something about these peaks, the two of them standing together, distant and austere. They belong to this world, and they don't. They're aloof and remote, mysterious and strange. They attract all kinds of energy and give back plenty of their own. It's not for nothing that the Aztecs made mention of them in their chronicles. They are our Olympus, dwelling place of myths and gods."

One clear, sparkling summer morning Barbara Sparks and I bounced uphill in a Ford pickup driven by longtime Spanish Peaks resident John Albright. John had generously agreed to take us to one of the upland pastures on the ranch owned by his son, George. On the way to meet him, Barbara and I drove south out of La Veta through a lush valley straight toward West Spanish Peak, whose stony summit glowed in the limpid morning light like a cluster of sculpted facets.

John Albright, behind the wheel of the white Ford pickup, guided us through a mixed forest of aspens and conifers. Deep in the trees we surprised a mule deer and two fawns, which skittered out of sight. We caught a glimpse of several wild turkeys, tails flaring, brawling like a bunch of drunks in a parking lot. "They've already hatched a brood," said John. "Now they're getting themselves riled up for another."

We swayed the grassy length of the upper meadow, through stretches of snowy white yarrow blossoms. Near the top, a few yards from the bulwark of a stone dike that bumped down from the west peak, he braked the vehicle to a halt and stepped out. He took his pistol with him, a .357 magnum, which he belted around his waist and settled on his hip. "What've we got up here, John, that you need to pack so much heat for?" I asked.

"You never know," he replied with a shy smile. "You just never know."

Mule deer, La Veta Pass.

John's a rugged, handsome fellow in his mid-eighties, still spry, still alert. Like most ranchers in these parts, he has definite opinions about things. After serving in the navy in World War II, he came out to the Spanish Peaks from his native Oklahoma to work as a pharmacist, then in real estate, then ranching. His face in the dewy mountain light was fleshy and soft, his eyes blue, his hair, concealed by a wide-brimmed Stetson, white as the fleece on a newborn lamb. He spoke with a gentle drawl and a subtle undertone of humor. He wasn't too keen on the proposed wilderness designation for the Spanish Peaks that was pending in the national congress. He didn't take kindly to strangers, and he didn't want them tramping on his land. He also didn't like the proximity of the federal government; part of his land already butted up against a national forest—the last thing he wanted was to deal with a new set of bureaucratic regulations issued by yet another federal agency. "The best stewards of the land are the people who own it," he declared. The twinkle vanished in his eye as if to underscore the gravity of his conviction. "We know the land best. We

make a living off it. It's in our best interest to make sure it stays healthy and strong."

Wild turkeys near Tercio.

John reminded me in many ways of my own father—contrary and headstrong, accustomed to having his way, tolerant and single-minded at the same time. My father and I used to get into some hellacious arguments about politics, and I think if you crossed John the same way, a similar donnybrook would follow. But for all his stubbornness, when he smiled at you or told a story—just like my old man—you forgot everything else just to bask in the aura he gave off. He could charm the rust off a boiler pipe, and he knew it, and like any special gift, he liked to spread it around for all the world to enjoy.

Barbara needed to photograph, and while they wandered off I tramped downhill, following the wall of the dike that snaked out of the treeless crown of West Spanish Peak and stairstepped toward the valley below. I walked for a while, feeling loose and giddy, exhilarated by the 9,000-foot altitude and the feathery touch of the wind. Western kingbirds worked the surface of the grassy field for fresh bugs rising through the warming air. The dike to my right resembled a medieval battlement, and I could imagine giants crouched behind it, ducking incoming boulders hurled by rival giants concealed behind the dike across the way. A notch appeared in the

"Wagon train" dike, Albright
Ranch.

wall, and I climbed up on it; below, a vast forest of aspens and conifers
swept laterally across the slope of the peak toward the boundary of yet
another wall a half-mile away. A fragrant morning breeze blew uphill, filling
my nostrils with the scent of moist grass. The grasses in this high pasture—
timothy, brome, bluegrass, and orchard grass—were all exotics, introduced
by early settlers along the eastern seaboard, transported by other settlers
through the humid valleys of the Midwest, across the dry plains to the
slopes of the Spanish Peaks, where they planted roots in new places, per-
petuating the cycle of renewal and regeneration.

The drop from my feet onto the top of the forest in the next valley was
probably a hundred feet or more, and feeling a little vertigo I stepped off
the notch in the wall, back out into the pasture. The pasture continued
downslope for several hundred yards, ending in a fence and a line of trees,
beyond which another pasture splayed out in a wide green swath. The view
from this perspective, standing in the middle of the field, was breathtaking:
pasture succeeding pasture, interspersed with groves of pines and hard-

John Albright, La Veta.

Notch in dike, East Spanish Peak.

woods, all the way down to the main valley, past La Veta and the Cuchara River, where the plains unfurled like a tawny flag to the edge of the earth.

I turned and started upslope toward the spot where John had parked the white pickup. A breeze rippled the grass around me in a smooth, gliding swirl that brought hackles to my arms and neck. The bald, rocky summit of West Spanish Peak loomed over my upturned face like a hairless head protruding from the cowl of a dark green sweater. It was all here, everything I needed, encapsulated in this field of vibrant imagery, a world of geography, culture, animals, history, human aspiration, and anguish. I could be content with this. I could live the rest of my life within this range—looking, listening, learning. There aren't enough lifetimes in which to learn all there is to learn about any given place. Each piece of information leads to a new one, and so on in a kind of steadily advancing frontal perimeter, like a coyote working a grassy field, winding back and forth, sniffing, checking, tasting, darting into shadows, back into the light again, across the rocky humps and promontories, tongue, nostrils, eyes sifting fresh signals and clues.

"Ah," I whispered. "*Ah!*" Since first viewed three decades ago, these stately, enigmatic peaks have beckoned over vast distances, tugging me across miles of cultivated prairie to these slopes where bucolic pastures

merge with unruly wilderness. *Wah-to-yah,* timeless source of thunder and rain, silent witness to so much suffering and pain, where spirits swirl and legends incandesce, where half-human bears still dance in imperfect circles.

Upland pasture, Albright Ranch.

Timeless beauty of the Spanish Peaks.

Bibliography

Adams, Robert. *The Architecture and Art of Early Hispanic Colorado.* University Press of Colorado, Niwot, 1974.

Albright, Zella Rae. *One Man's Family: The Life of Hiram Vasquez, 1843–1939.* Self-published, n.c., 1984.

Atherton, Lewis. *The Cattle Kings.* University of Nebraska Press, Lincoln, 1972.

Barker, Ted, Phil Leonard, and Bill McGlone. *Petroglyphs of Southeast Colorado and the Oklahoma Panhandle.* Mithras, Kamas, UT, 1994.

Benson, Maxine (ed.). *From Pittsburgh to the Rocky Mountains: Major Stephen Long's Expedition, 1819–1820.* Fulcrum, Golden, CO, 1988.

Beshoar, Barron B. *Out of the Depths: The Story of John R. Lawson, a Labor Leader.* World Press, Denver, 1942.

Beshoar, M. *All About Trinidad and Las Animas County: Their History, Industries, Resources, etc.* Denver Times Steam, Denver, 1882.

Brown, Lauren (ed.). *Grasslands: The Audubon Society Nature Guides.* Alfred A. Knopf, New York, 1985.

Brown, Robert L. *The Great Pikes Peak Gold Rush.* Caxton, Caldwell, ID, 1985.

Caputo, Silvio J. *The Death of Spring.* Ashley, Port Washington, NY, 1984.

Carson, Phil. *Across the Northern Frontier: Spanish Explorations in Colorado.* Johnson, Boulder, CO, 1998.

Chandler, Jon. *The Spanish Peaks: A Novel of Frontier Colorado.* Rodgers and Nelsen, Loveland, CO, 1998.

Christofferson, Nancy. *Coal Was King: Huerfano County's Mining History.* Self-published, La Veta, CO, 2000.

———. *Francisco Fort and the Early Days of La Veta, 1862–1876.* Self-published, n.c., 1987.

Chronic, Halka. *Roadside Geology of Colorado.* Mountain Press, Missoula, MT, 1980.

Clyne, Rick J. *Coal People: Life in Southern Colorado's Company Towns, 1890–1930.* Colorado Historical Society, Denver, 1999.

Cobos, Ruben. *A Dictionary of New Mexico and Southern Colorado Spanish.* Museum of New Mexico Press, Santa Fe, 1983.

Crampton, Frank A. *Deep Enough: A Working Stiff in the Western Mine Camps.* Sage, Denver, 1956.

Cummings, Lewis A. *History of the Spanish Peaks Ranger District.* Self-published, La Veta, CO, 1990.

De Baca, Vincent C. (ed.). *La Gente: Hispano History and Life in Colorado.* Colorado Historical Society, Denver, 1998.

Delaney, Howard L. *All Our Yesterdays: The Story of St. Mary Parish, Walsenburg, Colorado.* Consolidated Publishing, Pueblo, CO, 1944.

De Onis, Jose (ed.). *The Hispanic Contribution to the State of Colorado.* Westview, Boulder, CO, 1976.

Donachy, Patrick L. *A Rendezvous With Shame.* Inkwell, Trinidad, CO, 1989.

Dotson, Betty Jane. *Stage House at Apishapa.* Self-published, n.c., 1994.

Downing, Sybil. *Fire in the Hole.* University Press of Colorado, Niwot, 1996.

Drago, Henry Sinclair. *Great American Cattle Trails.* Dodd Mead, New York, 1965.

Drumm, Stella M. (ed.). *Down the Santa Fe Trail and Into Mexico: The Diary of Susan Shelby Magoffin, 1846–1847.* University of Nebraska Press, Lincoln, 1982.

Eastman, Max. "The Nice People of Trinidad." In William L. O'Neill (ed.). *Echoes of Revolt: The Masses 1911–1917.* Quadrangle, Chicago, 1966.

Eberhart, Perry. *Ghosts of the Colorado Plains.* Swallow, Athens, OH, 1986.

————. *Treasure Tales of the Rockies.* Swallow, Athens, OH, 1979.

Estergreen, M. Morgan. *Kit Carson: A Portrait in Courage.* University of Oklahoma Press, Norman, 1962.

Evans-Wentz, W. Y. *Cuchama and Sacred Mountains.* Ed. Frank Waters and Charles L. Adams. Swallow, Athens, OH, 1989.

Freiberger, Harriet. *Lucian Maxwell: Villain or Visionary.* Sunstone, Santa Fe, 1999.

Garrard, Lewis H. *Wah-to-Yah and the Taos Trail.* University of Oklahoma Press, Norman, 1978.

Grey, Zane. *Raiders of the Spanish Peaks.* Pocket Books, New York, 1960.

Hollon, W. Eugene. *The Lost Pathfinder: Zebulon Montgomery Pike.* University of Oklahoma Press, Norman, 1969.

Huber, Thomas, and Robert Larkin. *The San Luis Valley of Colorado: A Geographical Sketch.* Hulbert Center Press of the Colorado College, Colorado Springs, 1996.

Hyde, George E. *Indians of the High Plains: From the Prehistoric Period to the Coming of the Europeans.* University of Oklahoma Press, Norman, 1959.

————. *Life of George Bent, Written From His Letters.* Ed. Savoie Lottinville. University of Oklahoma Press, Norman, 1968.

Keck, Frances Bollacker. *Conquistadors to the 21st Century: A History of Otero and Crowley Counties, Colorado.* Otero, La Junta, CO, 1999.

Kessler, Ronald E. (ed.). *Anza's 1779 Comanche Campaign: Diary of Governor Juan Bautista de Anza.* Self-published, Monte Vista, CO, 1994.

Lavender, David. *Bent's Fort.* University of Nebraska Press, Lincoln, 1972.

LeCompte, Janet. *Pueblo, Hardscrabble, Greenhorn: Society on the High Plains, 1832–1856.* University of Oklahoma Press, Norman, 1978.

LeSueur, Meridel. *The Dread Road.* West End, Albuquerque, NM, 1991.

Lopez-Tushar, Olibama. *The People of El Valle: A History of the Spanish Colonials in the San Luis Valley.* El Escritorio, Pueblo, CO, 1997.

Lucero, Anne. *Trujillo Creek in Early Years.* Self-published, n.c., 1976.

Lummis, Charles. *The Land of Poco Tiempo.* University of New Mexico Press, Albuquerque, 1952.

Manning, Richard. *Grassland: The History, Biology, Politics, and Promise of the American Prairie.* Viking, New York, 1995.

Marsh, Charles S. *People of the Shining Mountains.* Pruett, Boulder, CO, 1982.

Martin, Floyd T. *Brothers Are Like That: The Martin Boys of La Veta.* Ed. Zella Rae Albright. Self-published, n.c., 1986.

McGovern, George S., and Leonard F. Guttridge. *The Great Coalfield War.* University Press of Colorado, Niwot, 1996.

McLelland, Catherine. *A History of La Veta, Colorado.* Saint Xavier College, Social Science Division, n.c., January 1961.

Moore, Michael. *Medicinal Plants of the Mountain West.* Museum of New Mexico Press, Santa Fe, 1979.

Mora-Espinosa, Deborah. "Teresita Sandoval: Woman in Between." In Vincent C. de Baca (ed.). *La Gente: Hispano History and Life in Colorado.* Colorado Historical Society, Denver, 1998.

Nardine, Henry. *In the Shadows of the Spanish Peaks: A History of Huerfano County, Colorado.* Self-published, n.c., 1987.

O'Brien, Christopher. *The Mysterious Valley.* St. Martin's, New York, 1996.

O'Neill, Floyd A. (ed.). *The Southern Utes: A Tribal History.* Southern Ute Tribe, Ignacio, CO, 1972.

O'Neill, William L. (ed.). *Echoes of Revolt: The Masses, 1911–17.* Quadrangle, Chicago, 1966.

Owens, Robert Percy. *Huerfano Valley as I Knew It.* Master Printers, Cañon City, CO, 1975.

Papanikolas, Zeese. *Buried Unsung: Louis Tikas and the Ludlow Massacre.* University of Nebraska Press, Lincoln, 1982.

Parkman, Francis. *The Oregon Trail.* Little, Brown, Boston, 1903.

Pearce, W. M. *The Matador Land and Cattle Company.* University of Oklahoma Press, Norman, 1964.

Pettit, Jan. *Utes: The Mountain People.* Johnson, Boulder, CO, 1990.

Ruxton, George. *Life in the Far West.* University of Oklahoma Press, Norman, 1979.

Simmons, Marc. *Coronado's Land: Daily Life in Colonial New Mexico.* University of New Mexico Press, Albuquerque, 1991.

———. *The Last Conquistador: Juan de Oñate and the Settling of the Far Southwest.* University of Oklahoma Press, Norman, 1991.

Sinclair, Upton. *King Coal.* Bantam, New York, 1994.

Smith, Anne M. (ed.). *Ute Tales.* University of Utah Press, Salt Lake City, 1992.

Southern Colorado Auxiliary of the Territorial Daughters of Colorado (ed.). *Pioneers of the Territory of Southern Colorado,* vols. 1 and 2. C.B.I. Offset, Monte Vista, CO, 1980.

Spenser, Emma Dill Russell. *Green Russell and Gold.* University of Texas Press, Austin, 1966.

Sporleder, Louis B. *The Romance of the Spanish Peaks.* O'Brien Printing and Stationery, Walsenburg, CO, 1960.

Tanahashi, Kazuaki (ed.). *Moon in a Dewdrop: Writings of Zen Master Dōgen.* North Point, San Francisco, 1985.

Taylor, Morris F. *O. P. McMains and the Maxwell Land Grant Conflict.* University of Arizona Press, Tucson, 1979.

———. *Pioneers of the Picketwire.* O'Brien Printing and Stationery, Pueblo, CO, 1964.

———. *A Sketch of Early Days on the Purgatory.* Trinidad State Junior College, Trinidad, CO, 1959.

Vallejo, M. Edmund. "Recollections of the Colorado Coal Strike, 1913–1914." In Vincent C. de Baca (ed.). *La Gente: Hispano History and Life in Colorado.* Colorado Historical Society, Denver, 1998.

Vories, Eugene C. *The La Veta Posse.* Exposition, Hicksville, NY, 1974.

Waters, Frank. *Mountain Dialogues.* Swallow, Athens, OH, 1981.

———. *People of the Valley.* Swallow, Chicago, 1969.

Webb, Walter Prescott. *The Great Plains.* Grossett and Dunlap, New York, 1971.

Weber, David J. *The Taos Trappers: The Fur Trade in the Far Southwest, 1540–1846.* University of Oklahoma Press, Norman, 1971.

Weigle, Marta. *The Penitentes of the Southwest.* Ancient City, Santa Fe, NM, 1970.

——— (ed.). *Hispanic Arts and Ethnohistory in the Southwest.* Ancient City, Santa Fe, NM, 1983.

West, Elliott. *The Way to the West: Essays on the Central Plains.* University of New Mexico Press, Albuquerque, 1995.

Wilson, Elinor. *Jim Beckwourth: Black Mountain Man and War Chief of the Crows.* University of Oklahoma Press, Norman, 1972.

Wilson, Raymond. *Biographical Sketches: Colonel John M. Francisco, Hiram Vasquez, Henry Daigre.* Huerfano County Historical Society, Walsenburg, CO, n.d.

Wolf, Tom. *Colorado's Sangre de Cristo Mountains.* University Press of Colorado, Niwot, 1995.

Wroth, William (ed.). *Ute Indian Arts and Culture: From Prehistory to the New Millennium.* Taylor Museum of the Colorado Springs Fine Arts Center, Colorado Springs, CO, 2000.

About the Authors

Conger Beasley Jr. is the author of *We Are a People in This World: The Lakota Sioux and the Massacre at Wounded Knee,* which won the Western Writers of America Spur Award for the best contemporary nonfiction book published in 1995. He has published two novels, two volumes of poetry, and a pair of short-story collections. He has written about Colorado in an earlier book, *Colorado Close-up* (Fulcrum, 1996).

Barbara Sparks has photographed in Turkey and the Himalayas. *Spanish Peaks: Land and Legends* is her third publication. Previously, she has collaborated with Ann Zwinger (*Aspen: Blazon of the High Country,* 1991) and Tom Wolf (*Colorado's Sangre de Cristo Mountains,* 1995). Her photography can be seen in museums and galleries in New Mexico and Colorado. She lives in Colorado Springs.

Photographer's Note

We left in the predawn light to fly over the Spanish Peaks, an area we had been studying on the ground for a year. I was rewarded with crystal-clear light to photograph the dikes of these world-class geological formations. The erosion patterns on the two mountains were more striking than anticipated. I used a sky filter, a 50 mm lens, and a 100 mm lens while photographing from the air.

On the ground I carried two Olympus OMI camera bodies, one for black-and-white pictures, the other for color film for a slide show in conjunction with this book. For the black-and-white photographs I used Ilford Delta film ASA 100 or 400, depending on the light. For color photographs I used Fujichrome 200 or Fujichrome 50, again depending on the light. Occasionally, I used a 200 mm lens and frequently a polarizing filter.

My favorite lens is the 100 mm, and I used it often, especially when photographing people. I have been fortunate in having a strong rapport with the ranchers in this book and finding open shade situations in which to photograph them.

—Barbara Sparks